BASTL

an introduction to the bastle houses of Northumberland

Julia Grint

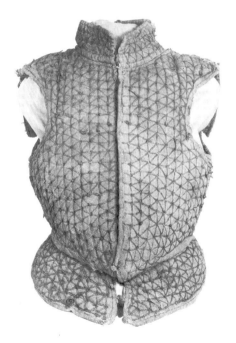

Ergo Press
Publishing for Northumberland

BASTLES
An introduction to the bastle houses of Northumberland

Ergo Press
© Julia Grint 2008
Photographs by Alan I Grint
Illustrations by Chloe Rodham and Rachel Pearson

ISBN: 978-0-9557510-2-8

Cover graphics by Slim Palmer
www.slimpalmer.com

ERGO
PRESS
5, St Mary's Chare
Hexham
Northumberland
NE46 1NQ
ergo.press@yahoo.co.uk
www.ergopress.com
Tel: 01434 689653

TABLE OF CONTENTS

Foreword

Bastle houses are an enduring feature of the landscape of upland Northumberland, evoking a troublesome past in one sense and yet forming an integral part of the character of the rural landscape. To understand and appreciate these structures is in some way to achieve an understanding of the social, economic and architectural background in this part of Northumberland.

This excellent guide to the bastle houses of Northumberland explains the hidden history bound up in these curious buildings, drawing upon first hand experience of visiting the remote and wild places where they have survived in close to their original form. It also provides a useful, accessible introduction to the social background of the bastle houses themselves and the people who lived in them.

With their thick walls and tiny windows, quenching holes and drawbar holes, the buildings are all about defence in troublesome times, but they are located in a landscape where ordinary people lived and worked the land. Many bastle houses can be found in groups, and some reveal evidence of other structures associated with them, revealing evidence of the daily routines of the 'reiving names'.

As one of the people responsible for the care and maintenance of the sites, buildings and landscapes of special historic, archaeological and architectural interest within Northumberland National Park, I am acutely aware of the need to increase people's understanding and appreciation of the historic environment. Publications like this are an invaluable source of useful information which raise awareness of an important part of the historic character of the area and enhance the visitor experience. This book contributes to the sustainable management of heritage and argues for the long term future of these evocative structures for future generations to enjoy.

Chris Jones
National Park Archaeologist
Hexham, 2008

The Charlton Spur

L egend has it that when the larders were empty at Hesleyside, home of the heidman of the Charlton name, the womenfolk would serve up at dinner not a joint of beef or lamb, but a spur on a plate. This was an unsubtle hint that it was time for the men to 'do a little shifting' – in other words, to go about their business of reiving.

The original spur and other relics of these violent times are kept safely at Hesleyside, which has been the family home of the Charltons since the 14th Century although the present hall dates from 1719. In Wallington Hall near Cambo is a huge fresco by William Bell Scott depicting the presentation of the infamous 'Charlton Spur'.

Author's Note

If you live in Northumberland and enjoy walking in remote places, sooner or later you will come across a bastle, ruinous or restored. This happened to me, and the encounter wakened in me an interest, then a fascination, for these extraordinary buildings. They are not extraordinary in a flamboyant way; indeed they tend to blend unnoticed into the landscape as do dry stone walls and ancient bridges. It is rather their intractability, their unsubtle and unrepentant solidity that makes them so wonderful: defensive yet domestic, apparently simple and yet curiously complex and adorned here and there, they compel us to take them seriously.

It isn't too difficult to understand the historical circumstances that made them necessary; my introduction offers a brief explanation of these. What is more difficult is to work out is how the people who came to need them knew how to build them: although they are (on the whole) constructed from undressed boulders and filling, as you will read there are features, notably barrel vaulting, which must have needed outside help from a specialist mason of sorts. Further, they are all different and yet they share a conformity that cannot be accidental. So who were the experts, and how did they come to 'design' this stalwart piece of vernacular architecture?

I am hoping that this introductory guide will ignite an interest that will make you want to go and explore the countryside and the bastles. To find those mentioned you will need large scale ordnance survey maps and suitable outdoor clothing, depending of course on the time of year. Before embarking on a bastle hunt, scrutinise maps of the region to which you are heading – in most areas there are other historical or pre-historical sites to see locally, some of which I have mentioned. Do visit the Northumberland National Park visitor centres and Bellingham Heritage Centre where you will find copious literature about such places, along with access guides. Please try to support local businesses as you travel, and walk rather than drive wherever possible; Northumberland's rural economy now depends partly on tourism, and you will find good food and friendly faces in the many tea rooms, farm shops and other enterprises along your way.

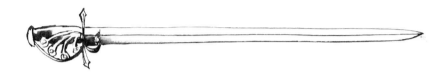

ACKNOWLEDGEMENTS

I could not possibly have written this book without the help of my husband and 'bastling' companion, Alan. Impelled by relentless enthusiasm he tramped with me through muddy fields, sometimes in what might be described as 'atmospheric' weather; he painstakingly took the photographs in this book and brought the whole thing together.

I must also thank those who studied bastles long before I did, whose erudition and research were invaluable. All of these are mentioned in the text and the bibliography, but my thanks go in particular to Peter F. Ryder, whose understanding of these buildings is second to none. Thanks also to my friend John Sadler, who loves bastles nearly as much as I do and who kindly read over the introduction with a keen historian's eye; his book *Border Fury* was essential reading.

This book is dedicated to my late parents, Tom and Dorothy (née Ferguson) Armstrong, both descended from reiver families. They loved their native Northumberland.

The wonderful original doorway to Old Town bastle may be seen from the roadside as you drive towards Low Bishopside. From the farm gate may also be seen astonishingly megalithic blocks which made up the lower courses of the byre, to the left of this doorway. If you park, please remember that this is a working farm. The square hole left through the doorway is for the hens!

Bastle Houses
of Northumberland

Wha daur meddle wi' me?
Wha daur meddle wi' me?
My name is little Jock Elliot,
And wha daur meddle wi' me?

I ride on my fleet-footed grey,
My sword hanging doun by my knee,
My name is little Jock Elliot,
And wha daur meddle wi' me?

In raids I ride always the foremost,
My straik is the first in melee,
My name is little Jock Elliot,
And wha daur meddle wi' me?

'Little Jock Elliot' (Border Ballad)

INTRODUCTION

Take a walk in the Tarset valley, a wild and sparsely populated parish in Upper North Tynedale; it is probably the best way to begin a study of Northumbrian bastle houses. Not much has happened since the 17th Century to alter the landscape and atmosphere of this remote and stunningly beautiful part of the county, and it takes only a little imagination to picture marauding reivers cantering across the land, intent upon their violent business. Fortunately, in these untroubled days, Tarset is the tranquil home of a leading poetry publisher and of some of the finest artists' pastels you can buy. Farmers may still struggle to make a living, but this is no longer because they live in fear of attack from their neighbours either side of the border with Scotland.

In other parts of the county there remains rather less to conjure up its harsh past; the landscape and domestic fortifications have, on the whole, been thoroughly tamed, as have the reiving families whose ferocity made them necessary. Nonetheless, in his gazetteer compiled in the early 19th Century, Archdeacon Singleton of Newcastle (1783-1842) described Haltwhistle as having some 'uncouth but curious old houses which betoken the state of constant insecurity and of dubious defence in which the inhabitants of the border were so long accustomed to live'. Singleton was describing *bastles*, many of which are now in ruins, others so changed that only a few original features can be discerned. In villages all over the county there are families living peacefully in homes that were constructed originally by men and women who were in constant fear of losing their stock and their lives.

Wall (near Hexham), is now as serene a village as might be by night, its quiet days are ruffled rather by the thrum of lawnmowers than the hooves

Stable Cottage in the centre of Wall Village

of reivers' hobblers; the shouting of lads playing football on the green shatters the stillness rather than the desperate cries of borderers suffering indiscriminate plundering. But Wall (named after that of Hadrian, near which it lies) was once a bastle village, its houses turned inwards in a defensive circuit around what is now the village green. Evidence of bastle features can still be seen in Greenhead House and in Stable Cottage, among others.

This book is intended to be a visitors' guide and introduction, with general information about bastles, and details and photographs of twenty that may be visited with moderate ease. I have included neither bastles that are inaccessible to the public, nor those that have been so much altered over the years as to make any of their original features difficult to visualize. The interested reader can extend his or her reading and find out details of every known bastle using the bibliography at the end of this book; those books still in print are clearly marked.

WHY BASTLES?

When England and Scotland were at last united under one Crown in 1603, the two countries had been at war, outright or simmering, for three hundred years, since the time of William Wallace and the Wars of Independence, which began in 1296.

William Wallace

Edward 1 of England

During the 16th Century there were further times of intense, open warfare between the two. Scotland had long been an ally of England's old enemy, France; indeed, in 1512 the 'Auld Alliance' between these countries was extended, and all nationals of Scotland and France also became nationals of each other's countries, a status not repealed in France until 1903.

In the following year (1513) this allegiance obliged James IV of Scotland to attack the English in support of his French allies, who had been attacked by Henry VIII (1509-1547). The result was the bloody Battle of Flodden, in which the Scottish king, many of his nobles and ten thousand men were killed – *The Flowers of the Forest* of the folk song.

James IV of Scotland

Henry VIII of England

Battle of Flodden and the destruction of Scottish nobility,
9th September 1513

Things did not improve over the century. After a period of regency, James V of Scotland succeeded his father and was married twice, the second time to a French noblewoman, Mary of Guise, mother of his only child to survive infancy, a daughter, Mary. In 1542 James' army was defeated at the Battle of Solway Moss in another disastrous campaign against the English; he died shortly afterwards. Henry VIII failed in his ensuing military attempt to win the hand of James' young daughter Mary (to be Queen of Scots) for his son Edward (to be Edward VI) – the so-called *Rough Wooing* that continued into the regency that followed Henry's own death in 1547. Adding insult to injury, Mary had been sent to France, aged five, as the intended bride of the French Dauphin.

The subsequent troubled history of England and Scotland, with Mary Queen of Scots (right) and her mother as key players, is well rehearsed elsewhere. From the point of view of the emergence of *bastle houses*, what is important is that the relationship between the two countries was perpetually either of warfare or of uneasy and restless peace, which is no peace at all ....

> [T]he Border country … was the ring in which the champions met; armies marched and counter-marched and fought and fled across it; it was wasted and burned and despoiled, its people harried and robbed and slaughtered, on both sides, by both sides. Whatever the rights and wrongs, the Borderers were the people who bore the brunt; for almost 300 years, from the late thirteenth century to the middle of the sixteenth, they lived in a battlefield that stretched from the Solway to the North Sea.
>
> *(Fraser, p. 4)*

THE BORDER REIVERS

Essential to our understanding of bastles is our understanding of the society that built them. The land north *and* south of the Border was a region of families, known as *names*, groups held together by the most powerful of all bindings – blood. Thus, not only was Northumberland subject to cross-border incursions from the Scots, but also to inter-family raiding. Indeed, the Border meant little to the reivers:

> The raiders from Bewcastle, from Tynedale and from Redesdale were as much a nuisance to their compatriots as was anyone from over the Border. Indeed, at the time *compatriot* meant nothing and the Border did not count for much, for men who had made the place too hot to hold them on one side would flee to kinsmen and friends on the other, being "Scottish when they will and English at their pleasure", in the words of a contemporary. *(Ramm et al, p.68)*

Woodcut of a raid in Northumberland, from Holinshed's Chronicle

Reivers (from the OE *rēafian* – to rob) were not all outlaws, although some of them were. They came from all classes and backgrounds, having in common the ability to ride and to fight and the need to survive in a hostile environment. Marauding reivers carried out cattle-thieving raids with impunity, both across the border and on their neighbours, knowing that the rule of law simply did not apply in their homelands; it was an accepted way of life. Practising systematic thievery and destruction, they have the dubious distinction of bringing the word *bereaved* to the English language, as indeed they did *blackmail*, another reiver practice.

> By the sixteenth century, robbery and blood feud had become virtually systematic, and that century saw the activities of the steel-bonneted Border riders – noble and simple, robber and lawman, soldier and farmer, outlaw and peasant – at their height.
>
> *(Fraser, p. 4)*

Surprisingly perhaps, these reivers were not indigenous to the Borders. During the 14th Century, in an attempt to repopulate an area made a dangerous economic desert by Anglo-Scots warfare, Edward III of England encouraged what we would term 'relocation' to the border region. The people were chosen quite deliberately as being capable of brutish and violent behaviour; the settlers were brought in to form a protective 'pale' or bulwark and needed to be suitable for that purpose.

In exchange for land and low rents the monarch required military service on demand: during times of conscription by his country, the reivers would serve as *hobilers*, light horsemen with considerable skill at reconnoitering and armed engagement. The area soon became heavily populated, a situation exacerbated by the *gavelkind* inheritance system, which on his death divided a man's land between his sons; the parcels of land thus handed down were too small to provide an honest living:

> This state of affairs, combined with a lack of legitimate alternative occupations, soon gave rise to an ever-growing delinquent element in Border society. Theft became endemic …
>
> *(Durham, p.5)*

So, an idea that had appeared to have merit went seriously awry. Like Frankenstein's creature, it developed a life of its own, with disastrous effects. These rough incomers established what we know as reiver practices and made the border into an area that John Sadler in his authoritative book *Border Fury*, likens to war torn Bosnia in the 1990s. The unique provenance and nature of the reivers probably accounts for the need for defensive buildings along this border; no such building for domestic protection appears on the Anglo-Welsh border. It is important to recognize that the people who built the bastles were the same people that attacked the homes of others:

> [A]lthough they were cattle-stealers when the opportunity offered, [these men] were for most of the time farmers, and not very different from the men they robbed … Thus they had as much need as their victims for buildings which would hold them and their stock in safety.
>
> *(Ramm et al, p.70)*

In other words, we are not talking here about a set of villains who were perpetually attacking their peace-loving countrymen. Reiving was the principal business of everyone in the region; it was simply a way of earning a living during the reiving 'season' of late August to February whenever the weather and skies allowed. As John Sadler describes:

> A foray might involve a dozen riders or half a thousand, with the graynes*
> active every night the weather allowed, the bright reivers' moon their

guiding star. So important was this lunar conspiracy that the image appears in border heraldry – the Scotts' badge was a star and two crescent moons; mottoes such as 'we'll have moonlight again' were popular amongst riding names.

(Sadler, p. 553)   * see below, *Names and Graynes*

No wonder, then, that bastles came into being.

Although this dangerous environment explains to some extent why bastles were built, it is nonetheless noteworthy that, as Ramm et al state, generally 'men below gentry level in the northern countryside could not afford to build good houses of stone or timber before the late 17th Century'. In other words they are an anomaly, in that apart from bastles there are no extant substantial vernacular homes built by ordinary countrymen in the area, whereas in the South of England there are many.

There are other explanations for bastles other than simple exigency, and these are put forward tentatively by Ramm et al. First, the need for protection made the bastle-owners ready to make great sacrifices of labour and wealth to build them, but this raises the question as to how they came to have such resources when, for most peasant farmers at the time, extra money was scarce. The answer lies partly in the fact that this was a 'period of transition between feudal power and effective state power' (Ryder 1992, p. 370). The 'family' system of the Borders (see below, *Names and Graynes*) may well have resulted in members paying smaller rents to their chiefs than was usual with peasants and feudal lords, and even when this did not apply, other local tenants were claiming that they held their land by 'border tenant-right' which amounted 'almost to a freehold'. This border tenant-right was challenged by landowners such as the Earl of Northumberland and William Howard of Naworth, but such was their power that from 1603, after a battle of over twenty years, the tenants were able 'in the end, to wring important concessions from them' (Ramm et al, p. 71). Further, there were many families along the Border who were tenants on royal land, and there is evidence that the Crown 'had allowed many of its former revenues to collapse'; in 1604 many tenants were actually paying the same or less rent than was being paid for the same land around 1500, and 'in real terms the drop was enormous' (Ramm et al, ibid). Thus, many of the people who built bastles did so because they needed to *and* they could afford to do so.

DISTRIBUTION

The majority of bastles were built within twenty miles of the Border between England and Scotland. Indeed Ramm et al claim that 'all of the surviving examples' fall in this area, and that the 'southernmost limit of distribution runs closely parallel with it'. This is explained partly by an Act passed in 1555 (in the time of Mary Tudor) which required 'castles and forts to be repaired and open ground enclosed with ditches and quick-set hedges in order to impede the movement of raiders' (Ramm et al, p. 63). However, Peter Ryder points out (Ryder 1992, p. 370) that more recent research has demonstrated that in fact there are known bastles well beyond the twenty mile limit, including those in Allendale, around Alston in Cumbria and in Weardale.

NAMES AND GRAYNES

Although the term 'clan' is widely used, the correct label south of the Border for the kinship groups referred to is '*surname*' or '*name*'. They were groups of people of the same extended family drawn together for self protection during the years of chronic insecurity. Names would feud

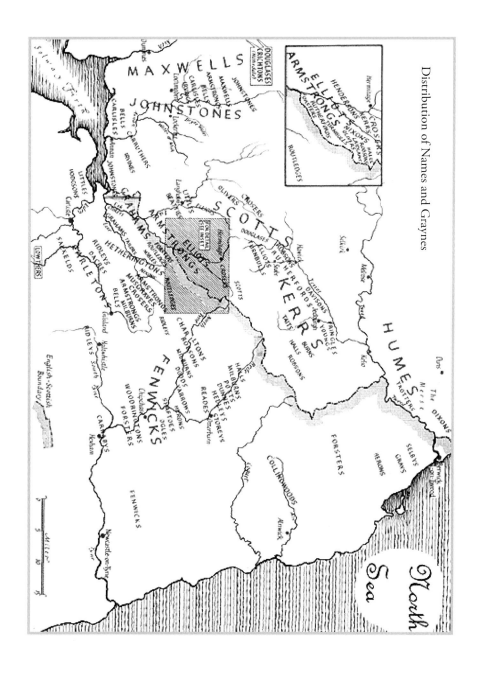

Distribution of Names and Graynes

with other names, tit for tat retaliation being common. The *graynes* were subgroups of the surnames, made up of a particular lineage of a name, with the entire surname having as its head (or *heidsman*) the leading member of the senior grayne. For example, the head of the Charlton grayne of Hesleyside near Bellingham was the recognized leader of that surname. Even a casual glance at a local directory will show that descendents of reiving families live here still, the names live on throughout the county: Armstrongs, Robsons, Fenwicks, Simpsons, Forsters, Grays, Croziers, Dixons, Herons, Cuthberts, Hedleys, Turnbulls, Halls, Ridleys, Humes, Elliots, Grahams and others, once reivers all!

ORDER ON THE BORDER

When we talk about the Border we are talking about a remote part of England, far away from the centre of power, difficult and expensive to police. A fairly complex means of trying to keep order was established as early as 1249, when the Scottish and English governments agreed that the border should be divided into six Marches – three on each side: East, Middle and West. From 1297 these Marches were controlled judicially and militarily by March Wardens. The Wardens were usually appointed from the south of the country, in order to avoid the obvious possibility of bias for or against the feuding *names* over which they were intended to hold sway; it was the Wardens' duty to see that peace was maintained, to administer justice and to deal with 'bills' or complaints. Backed up by a staff of deputies, captains and troopers, they tried with varying degrees of success to administer the law, but in doing so would create personal enemies (some were murdered) and further bitterness between the bellicose reivers. In short, they frequently caused more problems than they solved and most certainly did not implement peace and safety for the borderers.

One such Warden was Sir John Forster, not from the south but a native Northumbrian:

> A regular subject of Border correspondence, he was the target of frequent accusations ranging from collusion with the Scots and neglect of duty, to using his office as a cloak for thieving and skullduggery, his accusers further adding that Sir John's catalogue of shortcomings 'would fill a large book'. Most of this was in fact true and his protestations of innocence are somewhat less than convincing.
>
> *(Durham, p. 9)*

HOT TROD

C.R.

After a raid on a bastle, with the stealing of livestock and possibly the taking of lives if there had been a spirited defence, the reivers would naturally set off for the safety of home or hideout without delay. Above all else, success would lie in the speed with which the sortie and the getaway were accomplished. The reivers would be hampered by the spoils of their raid – cattle are notoriously difficult to move at speed – and it was essential to be familiar with every inch of the landscape so that temporary hiding places and strategic places for ambush were known and used with facility.

He who was left victim of the raid had three choices: to make a complaint to the March Warden, to bide his time until he could wreak revenge (with interest if possible), or to mount a *hot trod* (Fraser, pp 114-115). If some time elapsed before the pursuers set out it was known as a *cold trod*. Either way, the legality of the trod depended on its being within six days of the raid, and as Fraser points out, 'a careful line was drawn, under Border law, between a trod and reprisal raid'. If the trod was cross-Border, it was essential to make it clear that a legal pursuit was going on: a lighted turf was to be clearly visible on the pursuer's lance point, which was 'an earnest of open and peaceful intentions'. He had a legal right to assistance from villagers across the Border, and trying to prevent the trod was a punishable offence.

This said, the hot trod could be a bloody affair; however much there may have been strict rules for the manner in which the law was supposed to take its course, the trod frequently ended in a fierce skirmish during which fighters of either side might be killed, and 'the law was not likely to call a trod-follower to account if his rage got the better of him and he dispatched a reiver out of hand' (ibid, p. 116).

THE DEBATEABLE LAND

The 'Debateable Land' was a particular thorn in the flesh of those who tried to maintain the peace. First named in 1450, this small strip of land to the north east of Gretna caused a disproportionate amount of trouble, its distinction being that it belonged neither to England nor to Scotland, hence its name. Just as no power made claims to benefit from it, no power was in place to control what went on in it. The Scots and the English used it for grazing their sheep, but they also used it as a hideaway for all kinds of lawless activities and people. Reiving families such as the Littles, the Armstrongs and the Bells, along with the fearsome Grahams, felt free to plunder at will, taking little account of whether their victims were English or Scots. Wardens on both sides were infuriated by the lawlessness, eventually making a proclamation that:

> All Englishmen and Scottishmen … are and shall be, free to rob, burn, spoil, slay, murder and destroy all and every person and persons, their bodies, buildings, goods and cattle as do remain and shall inhabit the Debateable Land without redress to be made for the same.
>
> *(Durham, p.7)*

Eventually, the land was divided by the Scots Dyke, an earthen rampart, but their efforts did little to repress the activities and the villainy of those who remained there.

The Bishop's 'Monition of Cursing'

Church as well as state tried unsuccessfully to curb the violent and generally un-Christian behaviour of the Reivers. It is well documented that a visitor to Liddesdale, remarking that there were no churches, demanded 'Are there no Christians here?' and received the reply, 'Na, we's a Elliots and Armstrongs'. The exasperation felt by Church leaders was expressed in a most fulsome way in 1525 by the Catholic Bishop of Glasgow when he excommunicated all border thieves in his 'Monition of Cursing'. Surely the longest curse ever written it is too protracted to reproduce here in full, but the ending demonstrates the general flow:

16

And, finally, I condemn thaim perpetualie to the deip pit of hell, the remain with Lucifer and all his fallowis, and thair bodeis to the gallowis of the Burrow Mure, first to be hangit, syne revin and ruggit [then ripped and torn] with doggis, swyne, and utheris wyld beists, abhominable to all the warld. And their candillis gangis frae your sicht, as mot their saulis gang fra the visage of God, and thai rgude faim fra the warld, quhill thai forbeir thair oppin synnys foirsaidis and ryse frae this terribill cursing, and mak satifaction and pennance.

HOW TO RECOGNIZE A BORDER REIVER

A reiver looked nothing like a traditional knight in armour, although he did need special clothing and equipment to go about his dangerous business.

First, and most importantly perhaps, he needed a horse. Remembering that the borderers could be called up to fight for their king, their horses needed to be suitable mounts both for light cavalry work in time of war, and for raiding in time of 'peace'. Known as *hobblers*, *hobilars* or *garrons*, they were sturdy and fast, and like Cumbria's hardy Herdwick sheep they were cheap to keep. There is evidence that they were not groomed and that they didn't even need to be shoed. They were capable of 'transporting a man from Tynedale to Teviotdale and back in 24 hours' (Durham, p. 13).

Given the need (above all) for speed and ease of manoeuvre, the reiver rarely wore expensive armour even if he could afford it, which in most cases he could not. The preferred means of protecting the body was the '*jack*' or '*jacke*' which was widely used until the end of the 16th Century:

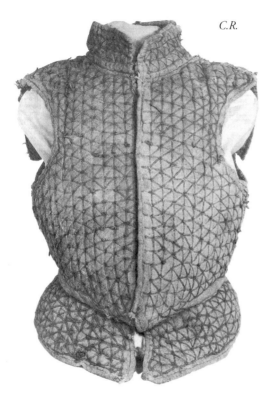

C.R.

[O]ccasionally worn over a shirt of mail, the jack was constructed from two or three layers of quilted cloth, twill or linen, between which were stitched small overlapping iron plates. Often cut from old armour and of crude appearance, these plates were between 2.8 and 3.9cms square (1-1½ins). Each plate was pierced in the centre for the cord stitching, which formed a latticework pattern on the exterior of the garment. It extended from the neck to the upper thigh and fastened down the chest by means of hook and thongs … Jacks were usually faced with a dense, heavy material such as fustian, canvas or stout leather.

(Durham, p.14)

To protect their arms and upper legs many reivers would use pewter or brass chains, wrapped around four or five times; their lower legs were protected by long, leather riding boots not unlike modern 'biker' boots. Dressed in this way, they were able to move quite easily but were likely to be unharmed by the slashing swords or daggers of the enemy.

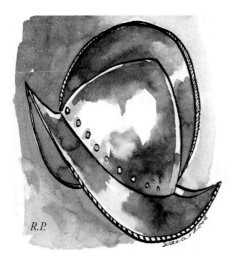

R.P.

On his head, the reiver would wear a form of helmet called a *burgonet,* in use from the middle of the 16th Century. The *burgonet* or *steill bonnett* was 'a rather more stylish helmet [than the earlier *salade hat*] which, in its lightest form, was open and peaked' (Fraser, p. 87). They offered good protection, having a flared rim at the neck as well as a peak at the front. In time (from about 1580) these were in turn largely superseded by the *morion* or *pikeman's pot.*

The borderers carried a variety of weapons. As Fraser points out, the 16th Century was the 'bridge between the medieval knights and men-at-arms, with their heavy armour and weapons, and the age of firepower' (ibid, p. 87). Most would carry a lance, used for thrusting and throwing at the enemy – and for fishing, too! There is a well attested record of them spearing salmon from horseback in the Solway Firth, testimony to their extraordinary skill with this difficult weapon (ibid, p. 89). Another favourite weapon was the *bill,* which had a spike, a hook and a single heavy cutting edge. A variation on the bill was the 'Jeddart Staff', made in Jedburgh; this was a slim 1.25m (4ft) blade set into a wooden staff, the blade having a cutting edge and a fearsomely dangerous spike. Both at war and on a raid, the reivers would use also a cutting backsword, a dagger and possibly a brace of pistols, although the guns of the time were highly inaccurate at a distance.

THE END OF THE REIVERS

Elizabeth I died on 24th March 1603, and by all accounts she was more than ready to die, having lost her youth and many of her old friends and advisors. Most of all she missed the companionship of her beloved protégé Robert Devereux, Earl of Essex, who had been executed at her command in 1601 for treason. Eventually Elizabeth, that feisty woman who had boldly claimed to have 'the heart and stomach of a king', seemed to give up the will to go on. Before she died she indicated that her choice of successor was James, son of her second cousin Mary Queen of Scots whose execution in 1587 she had reluctantly allowed, an event to which she referred as a "miserable accident". To James she wrote, "For your part, think you have not in the world a more loving kinswoman nor a more dear friend than myself, nor any that will watch more carefully to preserve you and your estate".

James I was determined to unite the warring nations over which he now reigned, although he met resistance from the English Parliament when he styled himself *King of Great Britain*. Then, as now, there were strong factions on both side of the border who were against unification, wishing to keep the two countries under separate governance, but the king's earnest design was to transform the international frontier into a heartland.

Over a short time the new king dealt severely with the state of lawlessness that had prevailed in what was now the middle of his realm. The Marches were abolished, along with the office of March Warden, and the region renamed *The Middle Shires*. The lawbreaking names were no longer able to evade the law, which was exacted with rigour and ruthlessness by the Commission of ten men, five from each side of the border, stationed in Carlisle. Many were hanged, often without trial (known as *Jeddart Justice*), in a long overdue purge. Entire families were sent into exile in Ireland, in particular  Johnstons, Elliots, Armstrongs and Grahams; indeed, to this day the most common British surnames in Fermanagh are Armstrong, Johnston and Elliot. Others were conscripted to fight overseas, in the Low Countries and the Bohemian Wars. With predictable, wily pragmatism, some reiving families, such as the Buccleuchs, 'reformed' and from poachers became gamekeepers – that is to say, they became officers of the law helping to hunt down their co-reivers, putting many to death. In return they were well rewarded with titles, land and property from their grateful king, who could with confidence assume that there would be no further cross border trouble from the Scottish king during his reign!

In any case, the reivers' teeth had been drawn: by law, no borderer was allowed any longer to carry a weapon or to own a horse above a certain value. Little by little, order was restored other than among the very dregs, so that in 1607 James I was able to claim that the Middle Shires had "become the navel or umbilical of both kingdoms, planted and peopled with civility and riches". In fact, this was a rose-tinted view because although peace and safety did indeed gradually become established, the old order took many years to change completely, especially in the more remote areas:

> By the 1640s what was eventually left was a hard core of 'lawless persons', being 'mosse-troupers, theifs and uthers wicked and lawless men', who, operating in well-organised gangs, terrorized the surrounding countryside by day and night with their repeated 'outrages, felonies and nefarious crymes'. *(Durham, p. 41)*

In his English Social History (1942), GM Trevelyan wrote with ambivalence about the reiving names, comparing them with Homeric Greeks, "... cruel and barabarous men, slaying each other like beasts of the forest, but high in pride and honour and rough faithfulness". In legend and song, reivers are often seen as rough diamonds "able to express in words of power the inexorable fate of man and woman, and pity for the cruelties they nevertheless constantly inflicted on one another". The truth about this era is perhaps better understood by stepping back into the time. There are many written sources which testify to the brutal and retributive behaviour of the names, the best to my mind being the Calendar of Border Papers which can be accessed (by subscription) via British History Online; letters to and from all of the major figures of the time are found here, such as the following extracts in Volume 1: 1560-95 (1894).

Border Complaints, 21 August 1582

Michaell Waules of Stewardsheiles in Ryddesdale, upon Arche Elwet of the Hill, James Elwet his brother, younge John Elwet of the Park, Hob Elwet of the Parke, sonne to James … Martyne Elwet of the Hewghouse called Red Martyne and their complices to the number of ane hundreth persons, for that they came to Eleshawe and there reft, stale and took awaye lxxx kye and oxen, vj horses and meares and howsehold stuf, to the value of xl sterling, a slew dog, and then murdered and slewe Roger Waules, the xxjth August 1582. Whereof he dothe aske redress.

Letter from Sir Symon Musgrave to Lord Walsingham, 25 January1583

Sens my sunne Christofer Musgrave dydde delyvver into the Qeunes Majestes jayole the iiij notabyll theffs of the Armstrongs of Lyddesdale, of whom thre was executytt, all dying to theyre deservings, thare frendes the Armstrongs of Scotland, with thier complyces, have nott seassyt to mayk incurtyons within thys ofes of Bewcastell, and have murtheryd many of the Quenes subjectes and utterlye spoylyd the sayd offes, so as the pore men are redy to departe forthe off the contrie.

Details of 'disorders committed by the Liddesdale men', requested by Elizabeth I, in letter from Lord Scrope to Lord Burghley, 2 August 1581

12 Julij 1581, complaint by James Forster, sonne to Adam. Upon thEllotes and their complices: xxtie old kie, xxvten old oxen, all thinsight* of his howse, and the wounding and mam-ynge [maiming] of Thomas Batie and Lowrie Forster Englishemen. (*insight was all of the domestic goods and belongings)

Ult. Julij 1581, complaint by Georg Armstrong. Upon th'Ellotes and their complices: xvten kie and oxen, one horse, all his insight, and his sonne wounded verie sore in perill of death.

Little here to be proud of, I think.

SITUATION OF BASTLES

As we have read, although by the middle of the 16th Century life in the south of England was becoming relatively safe and prosperous, the borders were fastened in the bitter grip of strife. Families in the area began to replace their old steadings, made of timber and earth, with relatively strong buildings made of stone; indeed, the availability of local building stone was one reason for bastles being built. On the whole it was fairly well-off tenants who undertook this work rather than their landlords – after all, it was families and cattle that were under threat, not the land on which they lived. For the reasons why the tenants could afford to build see p. 10.

As we know, these new, defensible farmhouses were known as *bastles*, a term derived from the French *bâtir* to build, as in *bastille*, a fortified building. As explained, the unruly and anarchic society in the Borders meant that the unification of the Crown in 1603 did not completely vitiate the need for bastles, which continued to be built for many years. Roughly speaking, they were built between 1550 and 1650, although many bear a later date which is the date of *renovation* rather than that of original construction.

They were not isolated buildings. Many had outbuildings, the remains of which can often be seen (as at Black Middens in Tarset), and they were often built in sight of other bastles – indeed they are often found in small groups. This would facilitate the alarm being raised and would enable those being attacked to have help from neighbouring families. Evistones near Otterburn is a superb example of a group of bastles. Some bastles were extended, a second building being built onto the end of a first, at the 'byre door end', forming a larger whole as at Housty and Monk Farm. In other cases, they were built in terraces, as seems to have been the case at Wall village, where the individual bastles kept their integrity although they were linked to their neighbours.

This may be a good place to point out that some bastles are known as *peles* or *peels* – Barty's Pele is an example. The words are often used synonymously, but the etymology of *peel* is from the French *pel*, meaning wooden stake, and is thus somewhat misleading when applied to bastles.

DESCRIPTION OF BASTLES

We have read that bastles were defensible farmhouses, and as such they are neither glamorous nor pretentious. Stark and roughly built, they stand as firm as if they had grown organically out of the very land from which they were built. They are utilitarian and austere, their beauty (if they can claim any) arising rather from the perceived romance of their history and their mighty stonework than from their architecture.

Bastle design, which varied little, became the standard for upland border farmhouses. Longhouses, which pre-date bastles, had the living area and the byre alongside each other; bastles altered this arrangement by putting one on top of the other. On the ground floor was the byre, into which cattle were driven when a raid was imminent and during bad weather. Without drainage or stalls, it seems unlikely that they were ever used for prolonged animal shelter. Above was the family's living quarters, which were without latrines and were necessarily simple. They had a fireplace at one gable end (usually the opposite end to the doorway).

Rarely bigger than 12m x 8m, bastles are rectangular and typically have walls between 0.7m and 1.3m thick, resting on a rough plinth of huge boulders set on the surface of the land. Dug foundations were very rare in bastle building (Ryder 1996, p. 7). They were constructed of large, irregular stone blocks; gaps between the blocks were packed with smaller stones (known as *galleting*) set in clay, or very occasionally in mortar (ibid). They have steeply pitched gables and some were probably roofed with heather thatching originally, although this was susceptible to fire, accidental or malevolent. Where the roof pitch was less steep (45°) and the timbers substantial, less-combustible stone slabs were used (Ryder 1992, p. 374). Most surviving examples have been re-roofed with slate.

Stone Barrel Vaulting, Akeld Bastle

Some bastles had stone barrel vaulting, springing from about 1.2m above ground- floor level, rising to support the second floor at about 2.7m. An example of barrel vaulting is found in Akeld Bastle, near Wooler, see also p. 117. Although Ramm et al claim that in Northumberland 'the two types [vaulted and unvaulted] occur in equal numbers and have the same pattern of distribution' (p. 65), this is disputed by the authoritative local historian Peter Ryder, who insists that this is 'quite incorrect' and that 'only about dozen vaulted examples (out of c.200) are known, and most of these are situated in the headwaters of the Rede or Coquet' (Ryder 1992, p. 372). Most had rough hewn, heavy beams to hold the second floor, and sockets for these are seen in the walls of many bastles.

The original flooring of the upper level of bastles may well have been wooden boarding, but it is clear that in many cases stone flags were set on heavy timber transverse joists, providing a layer of defence which would have been much more fire-resistant. Nine Dargue bastle in Allendale has the remains of such flooring.

Access to the byre on the ground floor was through a doorway, usually in the centre of one shorter, gable end and constructed from very large stone blocks. The design of the door way varies considerably, some being very impressive, with well dressed stone arches, sometimes chamfered and decorated. Sometimes the weight on a squared stone lintel was taken partly by the construction of a relieving arch above it. The relieving arch was constructed from wedged shaped stones, or *voussoirs*.

Many bastles had one or more deep tunnels in the jamb of one side of the stone doorway with corresponding sockets in the other side, to house hefty bits of timber which would have been placed in position to prevent unwanted visitors from getting in. These are known as *drawbar tunnels* and examples can be seen at Nine Dargue and at many other bastles. Some bastles had doorways with two doors and corresponding sets of drawbars.

door check

floor level
harr hole

In some cases *harr holes or sockets* may still be seen at the doorway, in the sill and (more often) in the stone lintel, marking where the pivoting *harr* fitted:

> Harr hanging is an ancient means of fixing a door so that it turns, not on hinges, but upon pins or an attached post that pivots in sockets in the sill and lintel. *(Ryder 1996, p. 7)*

The doorways would be rebated on the inside once or twice so that the door (or doors, often there was more than one) would close against a door *check*, which would prevent the door from moving outwards once closed.

Directly above the byre doorway was sometimes what appears to be a very small window but which was in fact the exit point of a steeply sloping channel in the wall (*quenching hole*, for a good example see Barty's Pele, p. 73).

> One account termed this a 'murder hole', but it is much too small to drop weighty objects on visitors' heads; its function must have been to allow water to be poured down, from some recess at first-floor level, to extinguish any fires that the said visitors might kindle against the basement door - the only accessible woodwork on a bastle a ground level. This feature was described to a northern meeting of the Vernacular Architecture Group

in the early 1990s, and various titles suggested. A show of hands made 'Quenching Hole' a clear winner. *(Frodsham et al, p. 266-267)*

View upwards through quenching hole

Windows on the ground floor would be (necessarily) narrow slits, or vents, for ventilation and a little light; they were small enough to have no need of bars.

30

Access to the second floor was usually gained internally by a ladder through a trapdoor, although a few of the 'better class' of bastles had a staircase within the thickness of the gable walls – Woodhouses Bastle near Holystone (p. 110) has an example of this feature.

View down through the deep hole in the barrel vaulting at Hole bastle, which was the means of access from the byre to the living quarters once the byre door was fastened. There is a modern trapdoor covering this today, as seen.

Many bastles also had an external door to the upper floor, set towards one end of one of the long walls, again reached by ladder. In later, safer times, external stone-built staircases were added. An example of such a staircase may be seen at Black Middens among others.

There were often two or three windows in the upper storey, but they were small and iron-barred; I know of no examples of original iron bars still in place, although their sockets may still be seen in many cases. Some of these winows also had shutters, for which harr holes can be seen in the stonework.

> As a rule the living quarters were lit by two windows in the front wall, to either side of the door, one at either end of the rear wall, and perhaps others in the gable ends. In better-class buildings these might have chamfered surrounds, but more commonly a heavy timber frame sufficed.
>
> *(Ryder 1992, p.372)*

The first floor living area was heated by a fire; the outline remains of fireplaces and their timber and plaster hoods can be seen in many bastles, as can hearthstones, or at least the corbels that held them. Some chimneys were set into the gable end of the bastle furthest from the door, the gable therefore being thicker than was normal. as is the case at Monk. At Hole there are the remains of an original fireplace, much altered over the years.

Other signs of the domestic use of the bastles can still be seen: 'fitted cupboards' were often recessed into the thickest walls. Sinks or slopstones were usually sited on the rear wall, some bastles still demonstrating a spout for drainage.

The cupboards were often found in the same wall as the fireplace, presumably because the heat from the fire would make that area dryer, and the wall was sometimes a little thicker.

Woodhouses bastle has one of the few original spouts to be seen. Waste water from the slopstone could drain from here. This example is immediately beneath one of the upper storey windows.

Some bastles had attics within the roof space, which would have provided extra sleeping accommodation. Ryder is of the opinion that this would have been the norm, the sleeping area being reached by a ladder and lit 'by small loops in the gable ends' (Ryder 1992, p. 374).

THE ALLENDALE BASTLES

The Allendale bastles are at a fair distance from the Anglo-Scottish border, and in the 1970 RCHM report all but a very few were not even acknowledged because, as mentioned in my introduction, it was thought that all bastles were built within twenty miles of the border. In 1992, Peter Ryder published a detailed review of the Allendale bastles (see bibliography) in which he states that it was in the 1980s, when a new review of historical buildings was undertaken, that the true picture emerged:

...a much greater number of bastles and allied defensible buildings exist than had previously been recognized; around 240 are now known across Northumberland as a whole, and thirty five in the parish of Allendale.

(Ryder 1992, p. 353)

Of these, I have chosen to cover six, selected for a variety of reasons explained in the text. Of particular interest is the preponderance of interesting doorways, some with beautiful arches as you will see.

HOUSTY BASTLES
HOUSTY AND HIGH CLOSE
NY836573
NY838573

There are two bastles at Housty that merit visiting for their features, but it is worth knowing before you go that these two were part of a greater settlement, a hamlet of sorts, and parts of a number of other bastles have been incorporated into stone walls on the farm. These two, however, are on public footpaths and are easily found; in my view, the round arched doorway of Bastle 1 alone makes your visit worthwhile. This bastle is quite close to the present 18th Century farmhouse and has been dated at 1625, 22 years after the Union of Crowns in 1603, whereas High Close is an earlier bastle, probably built in 1525, a full century earlier, during the reign of Henry VIII. Although any major excavations would involve a great deal of disruption to the peaceful lives of the family that now farms Housty, it is tempting to hope that at some point the entire settlement might be investigated.

HOUSTY

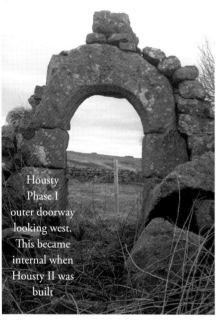

Housty Phase I outer doorway looking west. This became internal when Housty II was built

Housty is part of a small complex of buildings found on the right as you approach the farmstead, on the north side of a green or open area that lies between this grouping and the main farm, and it is certain that other bastles stood around the green, as mentioned above. This first complex consists of two bastles, one earlier than the other, plus an 18th or 19th Century byre, built end to end. It is the earliest bastle that is of greatest interest, because of its impressive doorway, which stands in the remains of the east wall (all that is left of the original building). The walls of this oldest bastle were about 1.2m thick; those of the adjacent bastle were 0.85m thick.

Little remains of Phase I to the west (left in the picture), apart from large footings in the ground. Phase II is confusing; the interior is full of huge stones, with one remaining original (rather wide) slit vent (seen oveleaf). The end wall of the 18th Century byre has been built inside the bastle, but the ghostly remains of the exterior Phase II bastle door are to be found on the inside of the later byre, as shown right.

Virtually blocked wide slit vent in Housty Phase II.

HOUSTY HIGH CLOSE

Housty High Close lies up the hill about 200m to the left (the east) of the farmstead, a five minute walk up the field boundary. This earlier bastle has obviously been very plain and is fairly small. Two venerable trees have taken up residence, and have undoubtedly caused much of the deterioration in recent years.

The doorway has a huge triangular lintel, so rough that it is difficult to tell whether it was dressed or not. Again, there are traces of other buildings close by.

If you continue up the hill after viewing the bastle, and through the gate at the top of the field, you will see a mysterious row of large boulders set into the ground; it has been suggested that this is an Iron Age boundary marker. Although this book concentrates on the age of the Reivers, it is always worth bearing in mind that there is scarcely a farm in the county that doesn't have prehistoric or historic remains of some sort. There are numerous closely researched and well-illustrated books on the subject.

How to find Housty: From Hexham take the B6295 towards Allendale Town. After passing through Catton Village turn left up a steep, narrow road. You will soon come to a farm track with a public footpath sign to Housty. Park here.
Access: Follow the farm track to the buildings.
Footwear: Stout boots or wellies.

Low Bishopside
Allendale
NY808582

It must be admitted that there is relatively little to see of the bastle at Low Bishopside Farm, but getting to it involves a pleasant walk with beautiful views, so it is worth the visit if you have time while you are in Allendale. Clearly there has been a lot of work done to halt the further decay of these ruins, which is good to see. There are the ruins of two buildings here, or rather one with a large extension. The earliest remains are at the east end, distinguishable by the thickness of the walls and the size of the building, which is quite small at 6.8m by 6m.

There is an inset on the interior of the east gable end marking where the upper storey floor would have rested; clearly the level of the ground floor has been raised by accretion of rubble and soil over time, not least since livestock will have used the ruins for shelter over many years.

41

Although there is no doorway in place, I found several large, roughly chamfered blocks of stone lying beside where the south wall would have been, one showing a single door check. Probably the door would have been to the upper storey if it was on that side. I couldn't find any trace of a door on what remains of the gable ends, although there has been quite a lot of collapse and renovation, so this is not surprising.

The size and construction of this bastle suggest that it is an early example. The extension on its west end is slightly later, but as you will see it, too, is very old – apparently a date stone showing 1657 from the building was reused in a later farm building. This date fits comfortably with the time that it became safe to 'come downstairs'.

How to find Low Bishopside: Follow the B6304 from Hexham to Allendale. Turn right at Round Meadows Farm before Catton, keep going west until T junction; turn left and then right after a short distance, direction Old Town. Stop at Old Town farm to view (from the roadside) bastle door. Keep going until you see Low Bishopside Farm on your right.

Access:

road).

turn lef

Footwe

This bastle is on private land and there is no right of access. A viewing can be made by arrangement with the owners by calling 01434 618331

NINE DARGUE BASTLE
ALLENDALE
NY 830540

Nine Dargue bastle lies in ruins, but they are *impressive* ruins. As I write, planning permission is in motion to renovate the bastle, and to convert it into hostel for walkers. This is a visionary enterprise indeed!

It stands on top of a bank in a field on the left hand side of a winding lane that also leads to a couple of other dwellings; it can be glimpsed through the trees as you drive down the hill. Its name is derived from the northern dialect word *därg*, a task, or day's work – a contraction of *dawerk* or day-work. 'Nine dargue' would thus refer to the amount of land that went with the bastle – that is, the amount of land that could be tilled in nine days.

As were most bastles, Nine Dargue was built in the late 16th or early 17th Century. It is rectangular, and three of its walls are a little less than 1m thick, with the east wall slightly thicker at 1.1m. The roof and upper storey have collapsed, apparently in the last century, (indeed, according to Ryder 1996, p.15, the house was inhabited until the 20th Century); nonetheless there are some interesting things to be seen.

Its main surviving features include a semi-circular (carved) megalithic lintel (pictured left) over the byre doorway, set centrally in the east gable end. Within the doorway are no fewer than three lintels, two stone and one timber.

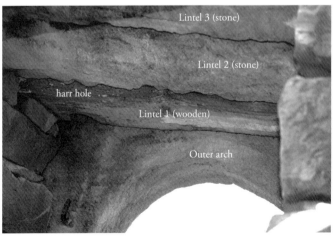

In the timber lintel there is a harr hole, here seen from below. It is also seen in the previous picture. Its corresponding hole at ground level is also clearly visible.

There are two drawbar tunnels. To the right of the lower tunnel can be seen part a much later door hanging, set into the original door check.

A mound of stones can be seen on the south side, indicating the site of an external stair which must have been added later, as is usual; when in position it would have blocked up a slit vent to the byre. The foundation stones are typically huge and impressive.

There are slit vents in three of the four walls. The vent on the north wall is unusually wide, although it seems to be original.

There is a curious chamfered jamb set into the south wall. It serves no purpose at all where it is, and must either have been recycled from an earlier building or to have marked an opening, now blocked, which to me seems less likely.

Particularly exciting are the presence of many of the fine stone flags that once formed the upper floor, resting on large transverse beams. Many of the beams are still in place, although they are much decayed. There is evidence that lighter timbers filled in the spaces between the eight greater ones, although they were too slight to have given any real support (Ryder 1992, p. 357). It was essential that a bastle had as little burnable material as possible, because lighting a fire that held was a sure way of forcing the occupants to leave the building, leaving themselves open to harm or capture for blackmailing.

Interior view of doorway

Stone floor flags

Wooden Beam

At the west end of the bastle, opposite the doorway, are the clear remains of the structure (corbelling) that supported the stone hearth, above a splayed vent.

How to find Nine Dargue: From Allendale Town, take the road north west to Thornley Gate. From Thornley Gate take the road towards Carrshield. At the first signed left turn follow road towards Acton; take the second turning left, which has curved stone wall on left hand side, fence on right. The bastle is down this narrow lane, in a field on the left.

Access: There is space to park down the road from the bastle, which can then be reached by walking back up the road and through the gate and across the shallow stream (Steel Burn).

Footwear: Stout boots or wellies, especially if it's wet.

Rowantree stob
Allendale
NY839512

I have included Rowantree Stob in this book for three reasons: first, it is accessible by a pleasant but fairly short walk across the Allendale landscape, and if you visit at a time when there has been a lot of rainfall it would be wise to wear wellies; second, it has a wonderful atmosphere and position, crouching on the hillside next to a burbling stream; third, it has a beautiful stone doorway. Unfortunately, the Stob is very ruinous and has been fenced off as a dangerous place to be, so even to attempt to see the hidden details would be dangerous.

The original bastle was clearly extended at a later date, so that the ruin is not a simple rectangle of walls, and is fairly overgrown. Thus, in most documents Rowantree Stob is described as having bastle features but having been remodelled, and to any serious bastle hunter this is immediately obvious. Apart from the much extended nature of the building, the walls are thinner than is usually the case (they vary from 0.6m to 0.8m) and it has the precarious remains of a tall chimney on the same wall as the doorway. Furthermore, the very situation of Rowantree Stub is hardly defensible: it is built on (and into) a slope so that 'uninvited visitors' could arrive unexpectedly – and dangerously.

However, it does have some typical bastle features in the oldest part of the ruin: the doorway is a classic, with a megalithic lintel into which a chamfered semicircular arch has been cut (see left). It also has a drawbar tunnel in the right jamb, but this cannot be seen.

There are two of the usual, narrow splayed ventilation vents in the lower part of the north wall, where the ground floor byre would have been. As mentioned above, the bastle is built into a slope, so that the external first floor doorway, which is in ruins now, must always have been at ground level to the south.

In the east gable, above the arch-lintel door, are three windows. The one to the first floor has a chamfered stone surround. Above, in the gable end, are two further windows to the attic (see left), the one on the right has a timber frame, the other (now partly demolished) had a chamfered stone surround.

How to find Rowantree Stob: From Allendale Town follow the B6295 direction Allenheads. At Sinderhope turn right. After about half a mile you will come to Pry Hill farm.

Access: Public footpath begins near the farm gate, goes through farmstead and the bastle is about half a mile beyond, near the stream in the valley bottom.

Footwear: Definitely wellies unless there's been a drought!

WEST SIDE FARM BASTLE
ALLENDALE
NY 790573

West Side bastle from the roadside

The bastle at West Side Farm is north of the West Side farmhouse, on the side of the road. One side of the bastle is on the roadside, the other can just be seen from the road; if you wish to look closely at the other side (by far the more interesting) it is essential to ask the permission of the farmer, because it is in his yard. The bastle has typical accommodation of the type: a byre on the ground floor and what were living quarters above. However, the walls are distinctly thinner than the norm, being only about 75cm thick. From this, Ramm et al suggest that this was a late bastle, built 'after the strict needs of defence had disappeared'.

The original entrance to the byre is in the long south wall, and as usual when this is the case, is not centrally placed but nearer one end, in this case the east.

Above this door a little to the west is the original entrance to the upstairs accommodation. As you can see, it is quite ornate, with beautiful chamfered jambs.

There are three windows to the south wall at the upper level, one of which is divided into two lights by a stone mullion. Ramm et al suggest that the windows are 'rather more generous than in normal bastles'. The window at this level in the roadside wall is a later addition.

There are also two small windows larger than slit vents at byre level on the south wall, (see one of these left), again suggesting that this was a later construction. Also to be seen is the boulder plinth of the bastle.

It appears that West Side once had attic sleeping quarters, because there is a window in one of gable ends at that level. Although this is not discernable from the outside, the interior has the recessed remains of a chimney in the west wall. The ends of the beams that once carried the fire hood are also evident about 1m from the gable wall.

On the north wall, on the road side, are two later doors with porches.

How to find West Side (or Westside): From Thornley Gate take the road to Whitfield, past Keenleywell House. West Side is on a corner on the left hand side of the road.
Access: From the roadside or (with permission) into the farmyard.
Footwear: No special footwear needed, although it may be a bit muddy.

Monk Farm Bastles

Allendale
NY783565

Bastle IV

Monk bastles are of particular interest for two reasons. First, they consist of a range of four bastle type buildings built in a 'terrace', and second, Monk Farm is believed to have been a 'cell' of the priory at Hexham. A cell was small monastery dependent upon a larger for supplies, with probably only two or three monks. Ryder suggests that it might have ɔeen "a house of correction", according to tradition. Whatever is the case, ɔertainly there was farm of some sort here when a survey was taken in 1547, the year that Henry VIII died:

> The earliest known reference to the farm is in a survey of Hexham Manor made in 1547, in which John ffalaker (sic) is shown as paying 12s.6d. rent for 'le Menke'. *(Ramm et al, p. 80)*

Not surprisingly on a working farm, the buildings have been altered a great deal over the years, but there are still some interesting features to be seen. Ryder (1992 p. 361) suggests that the building of these bastles probably occurred in a sequence from south to north.

Bastle III

Bastle II

Bastle I

BASTLE I

At the southern end of the range (the end *without* the dovecote) is what appears to the oldest of the buildings. It is roughly 6.6m square, and has huge quoins. Although it cannot be seen, having being blocked by bastle II, there is an original door in the north end of the bastle, with an unusual arch. There are several slit vents.

BASTLE II

Next is bastle II, which is slightly longer at 7.5m. On the west side this has a beautiful doorway, long blocked up, made of large stone blocks, the top having a rounded arch. On the other side of the building is a newer door and an original slit vent at basement level.

BASTLE III

Of interest in this phase of the building are the remains of a doorway to the upper storey in the west wall, which has a large triangular head. On the eastern side are original chamfered windows and slit vents.

BASTLE IV

This building has a dovecote which seems to have been constructed by adapting the original chimney according to Ryder (ibid), although Ramm et al suggest that this may have been a 'watch turret'. Of great interest is the byre door in the gable end, with its megalithic triangular head, which can be seen on the next page. On the east side are the remains of various original windows and a slit vent at basement level.

The whole of Monk is a spectacular example of extended building and rebuilding over centuries. It remains part of a working farm, and any inspection *must* bear this in mind.

How to find Monk: From Thornley Gate take the Whitfield Road. Roughly ¼m after West Side you will see a footpath sign on the left. Park here and walk.

Access: Follow footpath up the hill about ⅓m south east, then turn south west towards Harlow Bower and then Monk.

Footwear: Stout boots or wellies.

THE TARSET BASTLES

If you have time to visit only one group of bastles, I recommend that you travel beyond Bellingham to the head of the River Tarset, where there is a large and impressive cluster. There is plenty of help available here in the form of two designated 'Reivers Trail' walks with ample car parking at Black Middens and Sidwood (NY779889); walking between the bastles is fairly easy going, although the terrain and the distances do require a certain amount of stamina and surefootedness.

Begin at Gatehouse, which at one time was a strategic hamlet of bastles (there are remains of others in surrounding fields) but which has two fine examples remaining, both of which have been sensitively restored in recent years and which have retained many original features. John Dodds comments that:

> Plainly Gatehouse was the point raiding parties had to pass when en route for more prosperous parts of the Tarset valley, and similarly where the dalesmen would congregate before embarking on raids to north and east. It was the lodge at the end of the drive.... No matter that the inhabitants of Gatehouse were probably reivers themselves, they were fair game to the Scots, and also had to be prepared for violent retribution by past victims. *(Dodds, p. 296)*

It is essential to remember that these two bastles are privately owned and are not open to the general public, but the road passes between the two and you can easily drive slowly or pull up for a minute or two to enjoy the windows, stone stairway and doorways. North Gatehouse (on the right coming from Bellingham, with the stone staircase) is one of the best preserved in Northumberland.

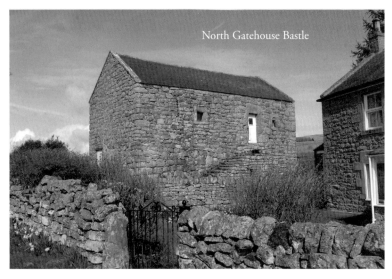

North Gatehouse Bastle

Interestingly, there is a legend – or perhaps it's true – that French prisoners of war were kept in the south Gatehouse bastle, in this case used as a bastille, during the Napoleonic Wars; apparently these unfortunate men were used as free labour by the powerful Charlton landowners nearby.

After Gatehouse move on to Black Middens, which has its own car park, and then to the car park at Sidwood to visit the other four bastles on the trail. In the following pages I have covered in some detail Black Middens, Shilla Hill and Bog Head. The others now have very little to show, but their importance lies in their *position*: these bastles were all built along Tarset Burn so that they could be seen one from the other. For example, Woodhouse (also known as Hill House), which is now a curious rectangle of grass-covered ridges, stands exactly opposite Black Middens, with the burn and the valley in between; in time of attack, the alarm could be raised quite easily from one family to another so that rapid help could arrive.

Curious remains of Hill House Bastle

Dodds relates a fascinating account of a raid in 1583 by the notorious Kinmont Willie Armstrong, whose forces attacked all six bastles at once, thereby deliberately vitiating this advantage. So savage and catastrophic was this attack, which took place in broad daylight, that the families between them wrote two letters of complaint to the Warden of the Middle March, outlining their losses. These included "fowre hundrethe kyen and oxen" and the murder ("crewellie") of six people, with eleven others "maimed and hurt". Others were taken prisoner so that the Scots could ransom them, using the blackmail of reiver practice (Dodds, p. 299). All of this serves to underline the tenuous safety offered even by bastles, and the dangerous times in which these families lived, giving the lie to the romantic gloss that has been painted over them by years of storytelling, particularly in the ballads of Sir Walter Scott.

Dodds cites the names and sites of *seven* bastles beyond Gatehouse, although the current trail has only five: Black Middens, Hill House (aka Woodhouse), Waterhead, Shilla Hill and Bog Head (aka The Comb or Barty's Pele). What very little remains of Waterhead lie close to the bungalow at the start of the Forestry Commission track. This bastle was the home of Jenkin Hunter, one of the men who wrote a letter of complaint to the March Warden following Kinmont Willie's raid; although there is very little to see, the bastle was occupied until 1851.

The sixth bastle mentioned by Dodds is Highfields. The ruins, the 'not very revealing jumble of stones', of Highfield Bastle are not on the Reiver's Trail but are at Highfield Hope, about one and a half miles away to the north west (ibid, p. 300), not at Highfield Farm as the OS map suggests. Although at some distance, Highfields was one of the bastles raided on that dreadful day in 1583, spelled as *The High Feeldee* in Jenkin Hunter's letter.

Dodds reaches a total of seven because he (I think mistakenly) makes a distinction between *Barty's Pele* and *The Comb*, as does Brian Long (p. 87). However, elsewhere these are taken to be the same bastle with different names (as was often the case, with the bastle being known both by the name of its occupants and by its position). In Dodds' and Long's view, Comb bastle may have been where Comb Farm now stands, although on Dodds' own admission it has 'disappeared without positive trace'. Thus, in Dodds' version of the famous reiver legend (retold here, see p. 76), Barty lived at The Comb and Corbit Jack at Barty's Pele.

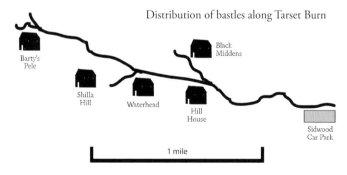

Distribution of bastles along Tarset Burn

Barty's Pele

Black Middens

Shilla Hill

Waterhead

Hill House

Sidwood Car Park

1 mile

BLACK MIDDENS
(MIDDINGS) BASTLE
TARSET
NY775898

Black Middens is one of a series of bastles that can all be visited in a single morning or afternoon. It's in the hands of English Heritage and is part of the 'Reivers Trail', so it is readily accessible, with its own small car park. Others bastles nearby of particular note are Shilla Hill (p. 70) and Barty's Pele (p. 73). This is a spectacular place to visit.

The bastle stands stark on the side of Tarset Valley, part of a cluster of buildings found at the site, which includes traces of another bastle and the ruins of an 18th Century farmhouse with enclosures. The building is of a standard size – 7.3m x 10.4m – and has large stoned, rough walls 1.4m thick. The roof is open, allowing good visibility from the viewing platform which has been specially constructed within the walls.

The south front of the bastle has two later doorways at ground level, between which there is a typical stone stairway leading to the original upper doorway, which would have been reached by ladder. Both lower doorways are wider than would have been the originals, being constructed, as were the stone stairs, in a less dangerous time.

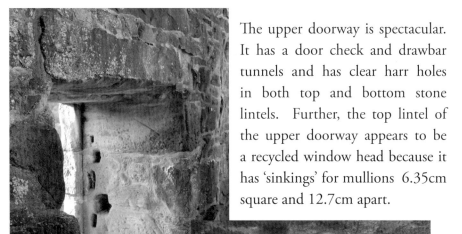

The upper doorway is spectacular. It has a door check and drawbar tunnels and has clear harr holes in both top and bottom stone lintels. Further, the top lintel of the upper doorway appears to be a recycled window head because it has 'sinkings' for mullions 6.35cm square and 12.7cm apart.

To the west of the doorway is a window with similar sinkings, although the smaller window to the east has no marks left by mullions or bars.

At the east end is the doorway to the lower storey, now sadly blocked, which has a lintel but no relieving arch; there are two door checks (now unseen); the doors must have been narrow and strongly barred. Also in the east wall of the upper storey are two cavities, presumably wall cupboards.

Exterior view of blocked doorway

At the west end is stone corbelling that once supported the wooden beams that held the stone hearth, which was typically in the gable opposite the door. The lower (byre) level was not stone vaulted; the floor to the upper storey was constructed with timbers set on an inset (see image), on which stone flags would almost certainly have rested. The viewing gallery rests on the inset on the south wall. As is usually the case, there are no remains of the chimney or hood in the upper storey.

There is a slit vent to the byre on the west gable wall.

There is what appears to be an original window in the upper storey of the north wall. The larger window at byre level is not original.

Of great interest are what appear to be the 'stumps' of the original roof trusses at the top of the north wall, although they are probably later.

The dividing wall in the middle of the interior of Black Middens is a later addition, probably contemporary with the new doors.

How to find Black Middens: From Bellingham, take the B6320 and pick up the brown signs for Black Middens

Access: Although Black Middens is in the care of English Heritage, it can be visited at any time and is free; there is a small car park.

Footwear: Stout footwear, or wellies in wet weather; it can be *very* muddy around the bastle.

SHILLA HILL BASTLE
ALSO KNOWN AS STARR HEAD
NY 763903

Shilla Hill with its bastle lies between Black Middens and Barty's Pele (Bog Hill, Corbie Castle), about half way between the two, both of which are also included in this guide; they can easily be visited in one good morning or afternoon. As was often the case, each of these bastles was built within (at the time) distant view of its neighbour, so that help could be called for in time of trouble. This is exactly what happened in the case of Corbie Jack and Barty Milburn, whose tale you can read on p. 76. In ancient documents, Shilla Hill was also known as Starr Head. Although Shilla Hill Bastle is in a deplorably ruinous state, there are interesting details to see.

The walls are of the typical random rubble with squared coins.

Shilla has an original doorway in the S.E. end wall, which still has a lintel on the *inner* face, although it has moved; the doorway has clearly shifted at an angle, probably because of pressure from the tree growing against the wall at that side within the bastle. The outer headstone is not in place. Just visible, cut into the full length of the huge blocks that form the sides of the doorway, are decorative lines a few inches from the interior.

71

At the time of the Royal Commission survey (around 1969) it was reported that Shilla Hill had a relieving arch in place, and the book has a rather fanciful line drawing to illustrate the entry, with a jolly piper playing to his livestock.

The door jambs have checks for two doors and tunnels for a drawbar. The photograph shows these features, and also the distortion to the doorway caused by the tree. Presumably the inner door also had fittings for a drawbar, which are now buried.

How to find Shilla Hill: Shilla is roughly half way between Black Middens and Corbie Castle, in Tarset forest. See Black Middens p. 65 for directions.

Access: The remains of this bastle are on the top of Shilla Hill.

Footwear: Sturdy, and waterproof in wet conditions

Barty's Pele
ALSO KNOWN AS
Bog Head bastle or Comb Bastle or Corbie Castle
NY 761909

The ruins of Barty's Pele lie 1 mile N.W. of Black Middens and a short walk from Starr. Whereas Starr commands Shilla Hill top, Barty's Pele lies in a hollow, these days hidden from view by trees in Tarset Forest, close to the confluence of Highfield Burn and Tarset Burn.

This was one of the few stone barrel vaulted bastles, although only the 'springing' remains; rubble from the collapsed walls and roof almost fill the interior. Interestingly, the ground plan of the bastle is not rectangular but is irregular, the remains of the north wall running at a slight angle from the west to the east wall that was a little longer, although this is not immediately obvious. A good slit vent can be seen on the back wall.

The entrance is in the west end, it is immensely deep but very narrow. It has dressed jambs and head with another stone lintel internally, with room for a third, wooden lintel in between. There are the remains of a relieving arch (one and a half voussoirs). Immediately above the apex of the arch is the outlet of the quenching hole.

Harr holes and door checks
for two doors

The jambs are double checked and there are tunnels for no fewer than three drawbars; one for the outside door and two for the inner, as shown. Harr holes for the two stout doors can also be seen, in the upper lintel.

The exit of the quenching hole is just above the remains of the relieving arch. Seen right is a view up through the quenching hole. The original 'entrance' has long gone, along with all of the upper storey.

There is a wonderful reiver story about this bastle, which bears repeating here. Naturally the details vary slightly according to which version you read, and I have used several different sources for my own:

> Bog Head was the home, it would seem, of one Bartholomew (Barty) Milburn, a powerful member of that Name. During one winter's night at the end of the 17th Century, Barty's sheep were reived by Scottish thieves. Barty immediately called up his neighbour, Corbit Jack of Shilla, and off they set on a hot trod over the border. They lost the track north of Carter Bar but, unwilling to return empty handed, they chose some Scottish sheep to replace those stolen ('Leatham wethers', which were best, according to Tomlinson).

> They had reached Chattlehope Spout when they were overtaken by two equally determined and sturdy Scots who wanted their sheep back, and hand to hand fighting duly took place in the long heather above the waterfall. Corbit Jack was killed and Barty was wounded in the thigh, but he managed to fight on to save his own life and to avenge that of his neighbour. He caught Corbit Jack's assailant a massive blow to the neck, at which, in Barty's famous words, "his heid spang alang the heather like an onion". Having also killed the other Scot, Barty set off home, in spite of his own wounds taking with him the sheep and Corbit Jack's body which, according to the custom of the time, he laid at his own door.

Even today, as you stand beside the burn, it takes no imagination at all to envisage Barty's return; his bastle is a worthy memorial.

How to find Barty's Pele: See Shilla Hill p. 70. From Shilla, continue along the forestry track until you see the sign.
Access: Easy parking and a peaceful walk along a forestry commission track.
Footwear: Stout boots or wellies

REDESDALE BASTLES

Redesdale is classic reiver country. A long river valley, it lies roughly between Otterburn and Tarset, close to the wild Scottish border, and was the stamping ground of the Reeds and the Halls. The north side of Redesdale is in the Otterburn Training Area (see Otterburn Bastles), although the bastles covered here are further south, not in a restricted zone.

Hole Bastle
Bellingham
NY 867846

This is a wonderful 16th Century bastle, part of a tenanted farmstead owned until recently by the Duke of Northumberland, overlooking the valley of the River Rede. It stands on a grassy knoll, partly covering a Bronze Age cairn, and can be seen clearly from the road. In the last twenty years the Duke has taken steps to preserve it, including the installation of lead flashing on the gables, but this does not detract from the integrity of Hole, which is a remarkable building. For safety's sake, a wooden rail has been added to the exterior stone staircase.

t measures 10.5m by 6.6m and has two storeys, three if you include he floored attic in the roof space, formed when the roof was raised. It neasures 14m to the tops of the gables.

It has a typical plinth made of huge boulders above which rough walls rise steeply to a roof that has been sensitively restored in recent years. On the long sides the walls have been heightened slightly at some point, in order to raise the roof; they now extend above the parapets of the gables.

Access to the upper storey from the outside is through an original door on the south side, originally reached by ladder, but to which a stone stairway was added later. The doorway has chamfered jambs and lintel. On either side of this doorway are 18th Century windows. Also on this side there are two smaller, original windows which were re-positioned higher up when the roof was raised. There are original windows on the north and east walls (easily seen from the road).

The upper doorway has a check for one door and drawbar tunnels. In the foreground can be seen striations in the stonework where reiver swords and daggers were sharpened.

On the west end of the upper floor is an old fireplace with a wooden lintel. The floor is typically flagged, and at the other (east) end is a small wooden staircase leading up to the attic. Wall cupboards are still in place.

The roof and timbers have been restored in recent years, but this attic area was clearly in use as the sleeping quarters. The chimney can be seen on the far wall.

The lower storey of the west end of the bastle is covered by a later farm building, so the original entrance there is blocked; the entrance built to replace it is on the east end.

The lower storey (byre) has impressive stone barrel vaulting, now used for storage.

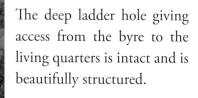

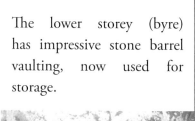

The deep ladder hole giving access from the byre to the living quarters is intact and is beautifully structured.

A BRIEF EXTRA NOTE ABOUT REIVING REDESDALE

On 6 March 1587, March Warden Sir John Forster was moved to write to Lord Francis Walsingham (of Elizabeth I's government) to defend his 'good' name, stating:

> In answer to your letter of the 1st, that information had been given to her Majesty of great spoils made by the Scots on her tenants, the Earl of Northumberland and others, which is laid to my negligence in winking at thieves and loose persons - I have never done so, but have always been ready to punish them and cherish the good .... As for her Majesty's tenants in Tynedale and Redesdale, they spoil others as they are spoiled, and suffer little harm.. *(Calendar Border Papers, Vol 1)*

It is well documented that Forster was a thoroughly untrustworthy and corrupt servant of the law, but to be fair, Redesdale had long enjoyed a reputation for wild lawlessness and venal wardenry. In 1498 the Bishop of Durham wrote an 'Admonition against the famous thieves of Tynedale and Redesdale':

> The majority of the inhabitants are represented as reivers and cattle-lifters, compounding for their offences by handing over a portion of the spoil to the venial officers of the crown, who both for clanship's sake and for the benefits received protected rather than punished the wrong-doers. *(Tomlinson, p. 297)*

How to find Hole: From Bellingham, take the road east towards West Woodburn. Hole is roughly 2 miles along here, on the right.
Access: Hole is close to the roadside, an integral part of a farmstead. It is essential to ask permission from the farmer to view the bastle at close quarters.
Footwear: Sensible shoes will do.

LOW CLEUGHS BASTLE
(WEST WOODBURN PELE)
REDE VALLEY
NY877867

Low Cleughs stands isolated on the hillside between Low Leam and High Leam, close to a fast flowing burn, or stream, a tributary of the River Rede; this no doubt was a reliable and clean water supply for the family and stock of the farmstead. It is well worth making the effort to view this fine ruin.

The bastle's walls are very solid at 1.4m thick in places, with large quoin stones and coursed rubble, and it is 13.3m by 7.5m, which makes it slightly longer than the average. Unusually, the doors to both the ground storey and the upper storey are right of centre on the same, long side (the south east) and are immediately one above the other.

Access to the upper storey would have been by ladder, and the curious positioning of the doors has precluded the later building of a stone staircase to the living quarters, as seen in many other bastles.

The lower doorway has a plain rectangular stone lintel and massive stone block jambs. There are two drawbar tunnels and checks, the lower check having been roughly enlarged at some point. Graham includes a photograph of this doorway, which the author describes as being "heavily marked with fire". The photograph is over fifty years old and this discolouration is hard to see clearly nowadays, but he seems to be very sure, claiming that the bastle bears the markings of the violence of the time:

Not the least interesting feature of West Woodburn Pele, however, is the sinister evidence it bears to its own ultimate fate. The ground-floor doorway is heavily marked with fire, as be can seen clearly in Pl. XII, 5; and the small stones that once filled up the interstices between the larger blocks have disintegrated and largely disappeared under the influence of the heat. Besiegers must have burned down the door, suffocating or roasting the people and animals within.

(Graham, p. 41)

The upper doorway has a beautifully clear harr hole in the upper lintel, as well as one (out of sight) in the lower; there is one drawbar tunnel. Ryder points out that "cuts in the internal face of the internal north east jamb indicate that a second bar could be dropped into position beneath the drawbar" (Frodsham et al, p. 304).

There were three windows to the south east in the upper storey at one time according to Ramm et al, of which two remain. These are well fashioned with a dressed head and chamfered surround. They bear the holes where iron bars would have prevented forced entry, although they are scarcely big enough for a child to get through. The window to the right of the door also has sinkings for harr hung shutters, as had the collapsed window to the far left of the door, this window may be seen intact on a photograph included by Graham.

Inside there are strong indications that the bastle was once in three rather than two floors, suggesting that this was one of those with sleeping accommodation in the attic. The first floor level 'set back' or inset where the floor would have rested, is very clear to see, as is that of the higher level of the attic flooring. Sockets for transverse beams to hold these floors can be seen beneath the set backs.

The short south west wall has the remains of stonework, across the full width of the building, which would have held the hearth, although there is no trace of a chimney remaining. Ryder comments that this south west end of the bastle had a firehood "which probably spanned the full width of this end"; the sockets for the timbers that held it up, below the level of the attic roof timber sockets, can be seen.

The attic floor space would clearly have been the smaller for the space taken by this firehood.   There is another window to the first floor, which is in the centre of the northwest wall; it is a simple splayed vent, without any dressed stone.   There are several cupboards with dressed heads in the upper stor

Low Cleughs door showing megalithic masonry and a rather wide slit vent to its left.

Frodsham et al have an entire chapter about Low Cleughs in its landscape including details of the entire complex of which the bastle was a part along with its history.   If you find your visit to be of interest, you might find it worth your while to read this excellent book, details of which may be found in the bibliography.

How to find Low Cleughs: From Hole Farm go east towards West Woodburn. After Low Leam Farm there is a designated car park on the left
Access: There is a clearly marked car park with information board. The bastle is a five minute walk up a moderately steep hill, alongside the burn.
Footwear: Sturdy, waterproofed in wet conditions

Otterburn Bastles

Otterburn is a huge area, remote and wild. I have included in this section bastles in Hepple which is part of this region. Four of the six bastles in this section are in, or are very close to, the Otterburn Training Area; access is simple and encouraged, but in a couple of cases you should check whether the red flag is flying. This is most easily done online by visiting the Northumberland National Park website (www.northumberlandnationalpark.org.uk) and clicking on *Countryside Access* then *Otterburn Ranges*. You should read the entire section, which gives some useful information about access. Alternatively you can pick up a leaflet in one of the Northumberland National Park Visitor Centres.

There is an excellent section in Frodsham et al (pp 324-338) about all of the archaeological sites on the Otterburn Training Area, written by Beryl Charlton. She points out in her introduction that this area 'boasts one of the greatest concentrations of multi-period archaeological and historical landscapes in the north of England'; there are too many to list here, but the remains include those of burial cairns, Roman roads and camps, bastles, limekilns and WW1 practice trenches. I can only recommend that you borrow or buy this excellent book if you wish to read about any of these sites.

SHITTLEHEUGH BASTLE
OTTERBURN
NY 869950

The ruins of Shittleheugh stand on a wind torn hillside to the north of the road from Otterburn to Jedburgh. It is a stone's throw from the Otterburn Firing Range, and if you visit on a day when exercises are taking place you could be forgiven for thinking that the shattered state of the bastle was caused by the army in recent years. A red flag may be flying on the nearby hill, and shots may well be heard, which adds to the atmosphere in some ways! There are beautiful views from the bastle across the valley of the Rede and the Otterburn moors.

The impressive gable ends project like broken teeth from the rugged hillside, and can be seen from the road at quite a distance. The long walls collapsed many years ago and the interior of the bastle is filled with huge labs of stone; the whole bastle was built with typically large blocks. The bottom part of the bastle walls are now covered by a venerable accretion of soil and stone. Nonetheless, there is much to see.

The doorway is (unusually) on what remains of the long south wall and is well preserved. It has two drawbar tunnels and slots. There is a door check to prevent the door from opening outwards. In front of the doorway are the much obscured foundations of a porch.

The top harr hole is very clear, although the bottom of the doorway is covered with earth and stone.

There are also foundations of a small building against the eastern wall, suggesting that the bastle was the centre of an extended, larger house. At a little distance, to the North West, are the substantial ruins of another building, although the walls are much thinner than those of a bastle. Altogether, the ruins of Shittleheugh suggest that it was a superior dwelling, and in his *History of Northumberland* J.Hodgson referred to Shittleheugh as "the mansion house of the Reeds".

As you wander round the bastle you will see well-formed vent slits to the ground floor, and a floor drain through the west wall.

Also on the west wall is stone corbelling which projects into the interior of the bastle (at first sight you may think that it is the remains of barrel vaulting), indicating that this was where the hearthstone once rested on the living quarters floor. Clearly to be seen also are the remains of the wall cupboards.

How to find Shittleheugh: Take the A696 north from Otterburn. Turn right at Greenchesters, drive about a mile north until footpath signs are seen on either side of the road. Walk to west until bastle is seen.

Access: Public footpath over fairly rough terrain

Footwear: Boots or wellies in wet weather, stout footwear in any case.

High Rochester Bastle
Rochester
NY832985

I have included High Rochester bastle not only for its own sake, but because it is near Evistones bastle village (p. 146) and Bremenium Roman Fort. In fact, all of the Otterburn Bastles and sites are within easy reach of each other, and you could spend many interesting hours in the area.

High Rochester is a hamlet with an open green at its centre. There were at least two bastles here, but there is more to see at the cottage actually called 'The Bastle' than at 'Rose Cottage' across the green.

The bastle has immensely thick walls (1.5m) and stands to its original height, although its roof is new and low pitched.

There is an original byre doorway, now converted to a window, with roll-moulded jambs and a lintel. In the south wall are a new door and the remains of the original first floor doorway, with similar mouldings to those on the byre doorway. There is a blocked slit vent to what would have been the byre, to the right of the new doorway.

On the north side are the beautifully chamfered jambs and head of an original window, measuring about 9 inches by 15 inches (22cm by 38m).

How to find High Rochester Bastle: Travel north from Otterburn on the A696, which joins the A68 at Elishaw. As you enter Rochester take a right turn to High Rochester. The bastle is on your left on the green.

Access: Plenty of space to park on the green.

Footwear: No special footwear needed here.

Raw Bastle
Or Haws Pele
NY 942980

One bastle and an infamous murder ...

The Raw Farm is aptly named. I travelled there on a witheringly cold March day, as blizzards swept across the bleak Otterburn landscape: it was not difficult to imagine the Spartan lives of the people who lived there and built the bastle. When I returned in April it was warmer, but the wet spring weather had meant a difficult lambing time for the Hall family; life here is no longer dangerous but it is still hard.

I am delighted to say that work begins in May of 2008 to restore this wonderful example of a stone barrel vaulted bastle, using public funds; the area immediately around it will be cleared so that visitors may park safely and view it properly. Currently it is well used for storage, as is clear in these photographs. The Raw is, and will remain, a working farm, so that visitors will need to display the customary amount of courtesy and consideration for the farming family. Until then, you can get a good view of the bastle from the roadside.

The bastle has been much altered over the years. A new door and window have been made in the west wall, clearly visible from the road. A stone staircase gives access to the upstairs, built when it became safe to do so, as was often the case.

There is a well built recess in the staircase, probably a kennel at one time. This is behind the right hand wooden barrier leaning against the stairs in the image above.

Raw has a tremendous barrel vaulted byre, the top of which may be seen in this image, which also shows a fairly large aperture which leads to a shaft; this may have afforded ingress to the upper storey. On the outside of the wall is a round arched entrance which leads into it, set low in the gable. To my mind it is too big to be a form of air vent (I could easily have squeezed my way in by stooping) although Ramm et al refer to it as a 'rough ventilation slit'. However, it is too low to be a doorway, and in any case there is an original doorway in the opposite gable wall. I am looking forward to finding out more as the bastle is restored.

As mentioned, in the other (south) end is the original doorway, now leading into a later building. It has chamfered jambs and an internal arch above it. There is a single door check, a harr hole and tunnels and sockets for two drawbars.

On the upper storey of the long, far wall, out of sight and perhaps likely to remain so because there is a well used much later byre built against it, is a most interesting feature. This is an original window which to right and left has two carved stones, each chamfered to make the jambs of the window, but then having strange carvings on their faces. To the right is a female human head, and to the left is what appears to be a rosette, with tassels below. It seems likely that these were brought from a still older (perhaps Roman) site when the bastle was built.

Ramm et al refer to the decorated window as the only original window, although there is one in the south gable that looks very old indeed, see left.

98

THE RAW, MARGARET CROZIER AND WINTER'S GIBBET

It is well documented that Margaret Crozier was a widow, a shopkeeper who lived at Haws Pele in the 18th Century. Apparently she kept a draper's shop, her customers being people who travelled along the minor tracks to avoid paying the turnpikes on the major roads. On the 29th August 1791, by now elderly, she was murdered by one William Winter, (whose father and brother had in former years been hanged at Morpeth for burglary, and who had recently returned from a period of transportation). He had been encouraged by Jane and Eleanor Clark, gypsies (or *faws*) who had previously experienced kindness at the hands of Margaret Crozier. Believing her to be rich, they took a donkey with them to carry away their booty. They were convicted of this dastardly crime in August 1792, largely on the evidence of a shepherd's lad who had seen them the day before the murder, and who had noted the details of Winter's boots and knife. They were all hanged at Westgate in Newcastle, after which Winter's corpse was gibbeted nearby at Steng Cross on Elsdon Moor. Gibbeting was the practice of taking the body of an executed murderer and hanging it in chains as it rotted, usually within sight of the place of the murder, *pour encourager les autres.* Because of tree planting it is difficult to tell whether at that time Haws Pele could actually be seen from Steng Cross, but it was a busy crossroads, with huge potential for effective gibbeting. The bodies of the two women were taken and dissected for medical research. The familiar replica of the gibbet, complete with a wooden head (or stob) is a ghoulish reminder of that time. After the murder, local people refused to live in the bastle, which then became a farm building, as it is today.

How to find Raw Bastle: Travel east from Elsdon on the B6341 towards Rothbury. After about two and a half miles, turn left at signpost to The Raw. The bastle can be seen on the right as the road twists through the farmstead.

Access: Currently access restricted, see text.

Footwear: No special footwear necessary.

High Shaw Bastle
HIGH SHAW FARM
NY935982

High Shaw sits on the boundary of the Otterburn Range; if the military access road above The Raw is barred and the red flag flying, it is wise to return on another day. When all is safe it is very easy to visit because it is immediately at the side of the road through a gate.

The bastle is highly unusual in a number of ways. First, it looks as if it may deliberately have been neatly 'cut off' at first floor level, perhaps because the upper storey was falling down and dangerous. Second, there is a narrow, chamfered string course (a course of stones projecting out from the exterior wall) where the ground floor stops short, which is unique in bastle architecture, suggesting that it was added after the demolition of the upper storey. High Shaw is constructed from typically massive stone blocks and is barrel vaulted, the surface of the flat 'roof' is covered with turf and shrubbery; it looks a little like a bristly haircut. What remains of the building is very well preserved.

The doorway is in the east (gable) end, and has a lintel and relieving arch; it has two checks and there are drawbar tunnels. Unfortunately this doorway is closed by a padlocked, barred gate, which prevents you from inspecting the barrel vaulted interior.

Access to the living quarters was through this barrel vaulting via a ladder hole which is about 12 inches square. This is hard to see in the gloom, but standing at the door it is to the right hand side of the vaulting, about a third of the way back.

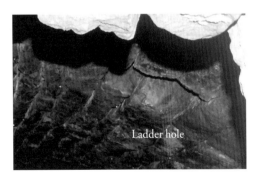

Ladder hole

Above is a view of the barrel vaulted interior of High Shaw. On the left of the vault may be seen the stone surround of a later doorway. The image on the right shows an exterior view of this doorway, which is blocked up. It is unclear why a second doorway was needed - perhaps the bastle was divided into two after the collapse of the upper living quarters.

There is also an unusual feature in the west wall: in the interior there is a coarsely made recess (between two small cupboards) leading to a vertical shaft in the thickness of the wall which can also be accessed through a well built triangular opening from the exterior. Ramm et al comment that the purpose of this feature 'is obscure', but elsewhere it is suggested that it is a gun loop.

The triangular opening can be seen and touched, but it is impossible to see the vertical shaft without being inside the bastle. As a matter of interest, Graham describes this vertical shaft as the flue of a "fireplace set about 2 feet above the floor, with the remains of a projecting hood on either side". In his view:

> This fireplace and the aumbry beside it seem to suggest that this basement room was designed from the first for occupation by human beings, not only by animals, and probably for more than temporary occupation at that. (*Graham, p. 40*)

It seems unlikely that the English Royal Commission would have failed to recognize a fireplace when they saw one, but Mr Graham's survey was earlier, and his assessment is interestingly unequivocal!

There are no obvious slit vents, which may suggests that they have been filled in leaving no trace. High Shaw has typical large stone quoins and a plinth at ground level.

View of High Shaw from the interior of Iron House.

How to find High Shaw: From The Raw (see p. 95) continue up the road past High Shaw farm. Take the military road up and then to the left (westwards). The bastle can clearly be seen, about 500m west of the farm, at the side of the road, just outside the limit of the Otterburn Range, although you will park within it.

Access: Very easy to park.

Footwear: No particular gear needed because of proximity to road.

Iron House Bastle
Hepple, Otterburn
NY933983

Iron House is much more ruinous than either Raw or High Shaw. There are very clear traces of a whole row of buildings here at Watty's Sike, best seen in a remarkable aerial photograph of the whole site on p. 329 of Frodsham et al, according to which the bastle was still occupied in 1753, and John Dodds points out that High Shaw and Iron House, although much deteriorated now, must have been in better condition in 1800, when the following notice was displayed on the door of the Presbyterian Meeting House in Harbottle:

> This is to give Notice that Highshaw and Ironhouse in the parish of Elsdon is to be Lett, Either together or Separate. Who Ever Inclines to take the Same may apply to Mr John Gallon who will Treat with them about the Same.

(Dodds, p. 189)

106

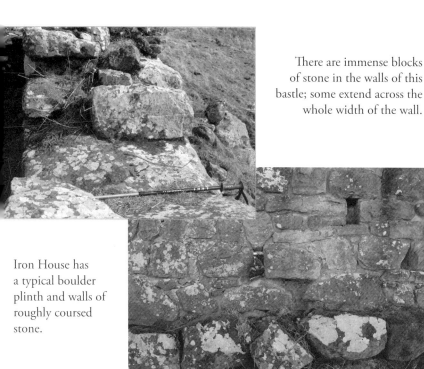

There are immense blocks of stone in the walls of this bastle; some extend across the whole width of the wall.

Iron House has a typical boulder plinth and walls of roughly coursed stone.

There is an original doorway in the south east gable, with a chamfer on the external lintel but not on the jambs. The doorway has checks for one door, with clearly defined harr holes.

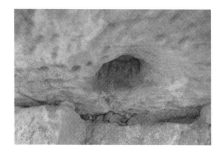

There are tunnels and sockets for two drawbars (see left).

The doorway has a small relieving arch still in place, above both the internal and external lintels which are of squared stone blocks. Between these may be seen the space where a large wooden lintel would have rested.

There are original narrow vents in the walls, see below.

Above: an interior view showing the relieving arch and the neat pile of rubble in the centre of the bastle.

In the gable wall at the opposite end to the door is a projecting stone which may well have supported the hearth. The corner of the building near this stone has collapsed or been dismantled, and appears to have been rebuilt at a low level to form a curved entrance for livestock. There is an offset at the level of the upper storey, and wall cupboards can be seen in each gable end.

The rubble from the collapsed walls of Iron House appear to have been piled deliberately down the centre of the bastle leaving a 'path' around the internal walls. It's tempting to wonder whether this was a rainy day job or an unruly squaddie!

How to find Iron House: See High Shaw (p. 101). Iron House can be seen to the north west, within the OTA. As you walk towards the bastle you will see a style over the fence.

Access: Please read Otterburn Bastles introduction.

Footwear: Stout boots or wellies, the terrain is rough and wet.

WOODHOUSES BASTLE
HARBOTTLE
NT 965004

One of the best known examples, this impressive bastle is much restored and is located south-west of Holystone Grange, where the owners live. There is a small car parking area and a permissive path, and although the bastle is kept locked you can see many of the details from the outside and can peer into the interior from various points. There are occasional group tours of the bastle, arranged in advance with the National Park rangers.

Built in the early 17th Century, it is constructed of typically coarse stonework and measures 11.5m long by 7.5m wide. The walls are 1.4m thick, becoming thinner above the vaulting.

Unusually, particularly in a bastle of this size, it had only *one* original doorway, at ground level in the east end. It is dated with the carved initials of William Potte, who according to records, held land here in 1604.

W.P. – B.P. – 1602
TAM

As you can see, the position of the relieving arch is unusual.

The doorway has a double check and has tunnels and sockets drawbars for each of the two doors, which can be glimpsed through the barred door.

Access from the byre to the upper storey was only possible via an interior staircase opening just to the left through this doorway, in the south east corner. According to Ramm et al this was probably a "later insertion and the walls have been reduced in thickness to accommodate it, but it was there before modern restoration was started". Ryder, however, is clear that the stairway was there from the outset (Frodsham et al, p. 267).

The image above shows the original doorway end (east) of the upper storey with the staircase emerging on the right, with its own window. Two wall cupboards can be seen on either side of a central window full of twigs.

There are a few windows with lintels in the south wall; beneath one of these is a stone sink (internally) with a drain to the outside that can be seen. Also in view are the sockets for two iron bars.

Woodhouses has a vaulted ground floor byre, typically used to keep animals safe, when necessary. The original fireplace would have been on the west wall, which has been partly rebuilt; it can no longer be traced and a later doorway is now in its place (see left). Beneath this doorway can be seen a slit vent to the vaulted basement. Above you can see the slit vent from the interior; it is unusually 'stepped'. This doorway replaced an earlier (now blocked) doorway to the upper floor, but it seems neither was there in the earliest and most dangerous days.

The bastle was increased in height in the 18th Century, when an attic was added. It was restored and re-roofed in 1904 and restored again in 1980s.

According to Tomlinson (p. 344), James Allan (or Allen), the celebrated Northumbrian piper, who played for the Duchess of Northumberland in 1746, was born at Woodhouses in 1734. In 1769 Allan was appointed town Wait (or piper) of Alnwick, but he was dismissed in the same year after an early conviction for stealing. The town Wait (Hexham, Morpeth and other towns also had a Wait) would signal the morning and evening hours along a prescribed route, or at a given location within the town.

He was of gypsy descent, and possessed all the cunning and roguery of his race. Licentious and dishonest, his life was one long evasion of the law. Condemned to death for horse-stealing, his sentence was afterwards commuted to imprisonment for life, and he died in gaol in 1810. Innumerable anecdotes are told concerning this singular character and his marvellous achievements.

How to find Woodhouses: Near Holystone, 1 mile north of the B6341, Elsdon to Rothbury road.

Access: The bastle can be seen on the hill from the road, and is easily reached by a permissive footpath from the car park.

Footwear: Stout footwear; wellies if it's wet.

OTHER BASTLES

The next few bastles lie slightly apart from the groups included so far, although every one of them has other places of historical interest nearby, including more bastles in some cases. I have mentioned some of these extra sites in the text, but it is worth stressing that Northumberland is covered in ancient places, so keep a look out as you travel. Staff at the various information centres are well informed and delighted to help, so it's worth planning your route to take in as much as possible.

AKELD BASTLE
GLENDALE, NW OF WOOLER
NT957294

Akeld is an area rich in remains, both historic and pre-historic: try going on to the *Keys to the Past* website (www.keystothepast.info) and putting Akeld into 'search the records'. For example, Yeavering Bell Iron Age hill fort is close by, near which are the buried remains of King Edwin's palace. Of much later interest, the Battle of Homildon Hill, a bitter defeat for the Scots, was fought near here in 1402. It really is worth allowing an entire day to explore this area fully.

Akeld bastle was first mentioned in documents of 1522, when Lord Dacre proposed to place ten men there for the defence of the border. Dacre referred to the building as a 'tower', but in 1541 it was referred to as 'a lytle fortelett or bastle house' in the border commissioners' survey. It is easy to understand why Akeld bastle defies easy definition, because it is much larger (55 feet, 16.7m long) and taller than most bastles, although its present impressive height is the result of extensive rebuilding, probably between 1170 and 1850, during which the granary and dovecote were constructed.

Akeld has thick walls (over 1.2m) built of random rubble stones from distinctive local, volcanic sources, with typically large boulders in the bottom course. The image (right) also shows a ground floor slit vent.

The ground floor is original and is impressively tunnel vaulted, (see below). There is an unusually small ladder hole to the upper floor, measuring 11ins x 14ins (28cm x 35.5cm), in the vaulting, now blocked with stones, see image opposite top.

The only original doorway is in the southern end of the long, west wall; its chamfered jambs have a double check and a drawbar tunnel. The doorway is square headed with a rough relieving arch, and is rather taller than usual. The plain doorway to the left (north) of this is a later addition.

There are several rough ventilation slits to the bottom, vaulted story. In the north end there are three in the lower part of the wall, then another higher up which (unlike the others) has sandstone dressings. Above these are a number of round arched pigeon holes, with ledges beneath on which the birds could 'land', leading to the dovecote.

The unusual stone double stairway and door to the upper floor on the narrow south wall are part of the 18th Century alterations, and give access to the granary.

How to find Akeld Bastle: From Wooler, continue north on the A697 to the junction with B6351, where Akeld hamlet lies.

Access: There is a public footpath that goes from the junction up through the hamlet and past the bastle.

Footwear: Sturdy shoes or boots. When we went there were lots of nettles, so beware.

CAMBO BASTLE
CAMBO
NZ026856

I have included Cambo Bastle (or Pele, or Tower) because it is in the lovely village of Cambo, very near Wallington Hall and Kirkharle Courtyard and not far from Belsay Hall, all of which are well worth the visit. Wallington Hall was originally built in 1688 by Sir William Blackett around an existing Pele Tower, and then rebuilt by Sir Walter Blackett in the Palladian style.

It passed into the hands of the Trevelyan family in 1777, after which it was put in the hands of the National Trust (1942); members of the Trevelyan family still live in the village. As you walk around Cambo, notice the 'dolphin' water fountain. The gardens of Wallington Hall were designed by Lancelot 'Capability' Brown, who was born at Kirkharle Farm which you will find by retracing your steps to the A696 and taking a left turn onto the B6342 towards Hexham after only a few yards. Kirkharle Courtyard is now the home of a fine Northumberland cabinet maker, many local products and an excellent coffee shop.

Cambo bastle was built originally in the 16th Century and has been a shop, then a post office, since 1818.

The bastle is unusual in that it appears to have been in three storeys from the begining, and is sometimes therefore classed as a *tower*. Before 1818 it seems that the ground floor was used as a hemmel or cattle shed, in true bastle style. In the south front wall of the bastle may just be seen the traces of an arch (four voussoirs, seen above to the right of a later window), which indicates the general position of the original door to the upper storey.

At one time there was an outside staircase leading to this doorway, which had an 'iron door' (Hugill, p. 52).

In the west gable are the traces of a small, blocked window (above), which is referred to in a curious story told by George Handyside, who lived in the bastle in about 1814. Robert Hugill quotes him:

> My father and grandfather had this shop before me, and before them it was kept by a warlock [i.e. a wizard], and people daursn't owe him anything! There was a woman lived where our kitchen is now, and she kept a cow, and when she churned she used to lock the door for fear the warlock cast an evil eye on the milk and turned it sour. His shop was upstairs, that's his window that's walled up.

As well as being taller, the building is rather larger than many bastles: roughly 8 yards wide (7½m) by 12 yards (11m) long. It has typical heavy rubble walls, four feet thick, and large quoins, "some of the lower corner stones being enormous", (ibid).

Dolphin fountain in the middle of Cambo village, not far from the bastle.

How to find Cambo Bastle: Cambo Village is near Wallington Hall. Take the A696 Otterburn Road from Newcastle upon Tyne; approx 5½m after Belsay, turn right onto the B6342 where signed. Follow the road past Wallington – the village is roughly 1m further along the road.

Access: Easily found in the village.

Footwear: No special footwear needed.

East Ealingham Bastle
Bellingham
NY846808

In this area due south of Bellingham, along the south facing slope of Ealingham Rigg at the 180m contour, are the remains of three bastles spread out over a distance of roughly three quarters of a mile. Furthest to the west is Lower Stobby Lee, or Stobby Lea, NY 838807 which is marked 'Bastle remains of' on map OL 42, then there is West Ealingham Farm which almost certainly replaced a bastle (Ramm et al, p.84). East of the farm is what is known as East Ealingham Bastle, marked on OL 42 simply with a small rectangle, then further east again are the grassed over remains of the fourth bastle, marked on OL 42 in the same way as Stobby Lea. Of these, East Ealingham has the most to offer.

The ruins of what was East Ealingham farm include this bastle, dated 16th Century or early 17th Century, as other bastles. The building measures just over 11m by 7m with walls about 1½m thick, except for the east end which is thinner. Despite some alterations to the original building, and its ruinous condition, there are many interesting features to see, including the byre doorway, which is in the west gable end.

This doorway has a huge rectangular top. Directly above this may be seen the rectangular exit of the quenching hole, one of very few to be found.

The interior of the doorway has two sets of drawbar tunnels; the image shows a latter day drawbar in position. There are some interesting striations in the stonework on the right of the picture. Perhaps they mark the place where knives and swords were sharpened.

Interior view of the west wall, showing the doorway, basement cuboards and cupboards in the upper storey (living quarters). I assume that the centre recess in the upper storey, above the door, was the 'entrance' to the quenching hole through which water would be poured.

On the north (right) wall can be seen the sockets for the timbers which held the floor to the upper storey. The door in the foreground (right) seems to be much later.

How to find East Ealingham: From Wark take the B6320 north towards Bellingham. At Bridgeford Gate Cottage turn left and drive towards West Ealingham Farm. The bastle can be seen in a field to the east of the farm.
Access: Walk across field to bastle.
Footwear; Stout boots or wellies

LINGY CLOSE BASTLES
NR LAMBLEY
NY685575

Nestling in the corner of a field, very close to a footpath, are the ruins of Lingy Close. This is a fine example of what is known as an 'extended bastle', by which is meant that a second bastle has been built onto the gable end of the first, so that stock would need to be driven through the later byre to get into the safety of the earlier. It is very much worth your while visiting Lingy Close for the wonderful views if offers of the South Tyne Valley, including the magnificent Lambley Viaduct.

The bastles at Lingy Close are built of huge, roughly cut sandstone blocks, and you can see a fine example of a boulder plinth.

The older of the two (Ryder 1992, p.22) is that to the north, furthest away from the nearby wall and style. It has an original door in the southern gable end, i.e. now roughly in the middle of the two bastles. The outer lintel is no longer there, but the inner is large and rectangular. There are the remains of a much later doorway in the western wall. In the northern gable end is an original (and standard) blocked splayed vent.

The second bastle has thinner walls, and its byre doorway is better preserved. Clearly visible are its rectangular head and a drawbar tunnel in the eastern (on the right as you enter) jamb.

It also has an internal wooden lintel, with clear remains of a harr socket for the original door.

There are very clear signs of internal walls in the second bastle, which would undoubtedly be inserted later, although it is unclear when.

How to find Lingy Close: As the A69 bypasses Haltwhistle, turn up Bellister Bank towards Park Village, then Featherstone Rowfoot. Go straight ahead at Lanehead crossroads and follow the yellow road to Tows Bank, where you can join the footpath that takes you north past Lingy Close bastles, which are not marked as such on the OS map.

Access: Park wherever is safest. Walk about ¾ mile north across fields past Towsbank Farm. The bastles are on the footpath.

Footwear: Stout boots or wellies.

Hebburn (Hepburn) Bastle
NU 070248
'Hepburn' is a relatively modern
reworking of 'Hebburn'

Hebburn Bastle was originally built in the late 15th Century and early 16th Century, but as was often the case it was modified over the following centuries, although what now remains belongs largely to the earliest period.   This marks it out as being older than a true bastle, and apart from its age it must be said that there is some discussion about whether Hebburn Bastle is modest enough to conform to the genre, or whether it should it rightfully be termed a tower.   In 1509 it was recorded as being large enough to hold 'twenty horsemen ready to ride', in 1541 it was described as 'a lytle tower' and in 1564 the owner referred to it as 'my mansion house'.   It has two gables, and in the survey of 1715 it was noted as 'a handsome house belonging to Robert Heburn esq.'.   All of this rather distinguishes it from more primitive bastles, but it is not really tall enough to be a tower, having only two storeys, and it has many bastle features. Dodds is adamant that Hebburn (he calls it Hepburn) cannot be a bastle, it being 'larger, more elaborate and better fortified than such a structure' (pp 104-5). My own view is that this building is of such Brogdingnagian proportions that it demands a visit, if only to compare it with its Lilliputian counterparts.

The impressive ruins stand just within the walls of Chillingham Park, to which the Hebburn family estate was added in the 18th Century when the local Hebburn family line effectively ended with an heiress. It can easily be seen from the road, and to the north east you can also see Ros Castle Crag, a sandstone outcrop on which once stood a famous beacon which was lit in times of serious incursion by Scottish reivers. In fact Ros was never a castle but was an Iron Age settlement. You are also on the doorstep of the magnificent Chillingham Castle and the unique Chillingham herd of wild cattle.

The tower stands two storeys high with well preserved twin gable ends to the east; less intact to the west. It is rectangular and measures about 16.6m by 10.8m externally with walls of well-tooled sandstone blocks. There is a very smart chamfered plinth at ground level and a fine chamfered set-back a little below the eaves. There are the very clear marks in the south wall (facing the road) of the pitched roof of the mansion wing, built in the mid 16th Century but now entirely gone.

At basement level, the walls are the thickest I have seen: about 2.7m. This is best seen at the only doorway, which is on the south side and which unfortunately is well barred. This doorway, which is dwarfed by the height of the walls, has obviously been partially rebuilt at some point; a drawbar tunnel can be seen on the right (east) side, but a socket was not incorporated in the stonework of the reconstructed left side.

The east wall is even thicker because it once incorporated a spiral staircase, now long gone but the space that it inhabited is quite clear – a huge, rounded gap in the south east corner, with a (blocked) arched doorway into the entrance of the byre (see above). It also houses a small, 'mural' room, to which there is an original vent in the east gable, along with what appears to be the ghost of a later, now blocked, doorway.

Although it's now frustratingly impossible to view clearly, there is a barrel vaulted basement with the remains of a later fireplace in the north wall. At the east end, a doorway leads to the mural chamber. Although this can not be seen from the exterior, Hugill describes that below this room is a small subterranean dungeon, again not a typical bastle feature. The first floor was divided into three rooms, each with a fireplace. In many of the early photographs of Hebburn Bastle the second floor, or attic level, is partially obscured by thick ivy. These days it has been cleared and some fine windows can be seen, as can those to the first floor. Some are mullioned, most were barred.

Blood feuds were common among reiver names – 'tit for tat' retributive killing that could go on for years. Dodds (p. 105) includes a story about a blood feud between the Hebburns and the Storys that deserves retelling here. It appears that in the 16th Century (our period) the Hebburn family murdered one John Story of the Story name. Far from denying all guilt, the Hebburns freely admitted the crime, but in their defence stated that the killing had been done with the agreement, indeed the behest, of the boy's father, 'Red' Martyn Story. However, the dead man's two brothers were unaware of this arrangement and established a blood feud with the Hebburns to avenge their brother's murder. In 1588, after the death of 'Red', both sides agreed to arbitration by Edmund Craster and Luke Ogle to bring an end to the feud. During the proceedings it became clear that 'Red' had actually paid 'certain sums of money for the said agreement', although the reason for this unnatural contract never came to light. Apparently, the arbitration was successful.

How to find Hebburn: From Chatton, drive south towards Chillingham Castle. Pass main gate on left, take next turning left, signpost Hepburn. After passing through Hepburn, the bastle can be seen very soon on your left in a field.
Access: Easy parking near field gate.
Footwear: Stout walking shoes.

BASTLE VILLAGES

As I have explained elsewhere, bastles were often built in groups, forming small hamlets or entire villages. Sometimes, as at Evistones, there is evidence that a 'curtain wall' was built between the dwellings, for extra protection and to hold any stock that wouldn't fit in the byres of the bastles. In most cases, such as at Housty or Gatehouse, the evidence for a much larger group of buildings is strong but the remains are scant. However, the two villages I have chosen to cover have a good deal to see, but in different ways.

Other bastle villages include Branshaw, which lies on Dere Street, the ancient Roman Road to the north. The ruins of this medieval settlement are on the OTA, at NY880996, with the bastle at the centre of the group of remains. At Wooley Farm in Allendale, about one mile south west of Allendale town (NY 828545), is a bastle complex, with some of the oldest buildings in the region. There are public footpaths taking you close to the farm buildings, which form a rough triangle. If you have the time and inclination you can also visit Chesterwood near Haydon Bridge, which is mentioned as a defensive village in many of the sources, although the experts argue as to the number of bastles.

WALL VILLAGE BASTLES
NY916690

Wall is well known for being a 'bastle village', although as mentioned in the introduction it is peaceful and tamed nowadays, with relatively little evidence of its reiver past. Nonetheless, there *are* houses that have kept some bastle characteristics and the layout of the older dwellings is still roughly as it was – a defensive circuit around the village green. As you wander round the village you may note that the houses include masonry taken from Hadrian's Wall, which of course lies only a stone's throw away. While you are in this area there are many interesting Roman sites to visit, including (on the way to Chollerford) Brunton Turret and then (past Chollerford) Chesters Roman Fort, the beautiful Chesters Walled Garden and further west again some wonderful stretches of the wall and Vindolanda and Housesteads. Within Housesteads Roman site is yet another bastle, a wonderful anachronism.

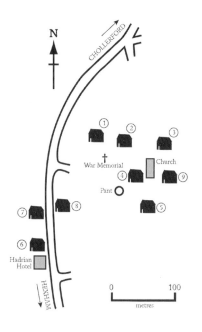

1   Greenhead House

2   The Cottage and
     Edges Green

3   St Oswald's Cottages

4   Stable Cottage

5   Town Farm House

6   Hadrian Cottages

7   Penrhyn

8   Orchard House

9   Fellfoot

Park in the centre of Wall; the buildings are best viewed by strolling around. Greenhead House (number 1) stands at the northwest corner of the village, overlooking the war memorial. These days it has a rather grand air about it, but close inspection shows that although much altered it was a bastle in its youth. Seen at a glance are its thick walls made of large stones.

The remains of the original, gently arched byre doorway can be seen very clearly to the left of the 'new' porch (see previous page); note that in this case entry to the byre was in a long wall rather than a gable end, probably because Greenhead was part of a terrace. Certainly the traces of another, perhaps older, building can be seen in the left (west) wall.

Above the porch are traces of the doorway to the living quarters, which would have been reached by a ladder. Also to be seen are blocked up windows to left and right of the porch, although these would surely be added later, perhaps in 1631 when times were somewhat safer; a stone with that date has been re-situated in the (much later) porch. The stone also bears the words, FEARE GOD IN HART, as does a very similar stone over the doorway of the end St Oswald's Cottage, (number 3). The earliest Greenhead bastle would almost certainly have had only slit vents to the ground floor byre, as described in the introduction and seen elsewhere. No doubt any traces of the original upstairs windows were destroyed when much larger and later windows were installed.

Walking from Greenhead House towards the church you will see The Cottage (number 2), once a bastle, which although much altered is easily recognizable by its masonry and its blocked slit vent. This is terraced with Edges Green, which has a new front wall; apparently the original wall fell down during the removal of an ancient fireplace. Both have enormously thick walls and were undoubtedly bastles.

Further along again in a more-or less straight line, passing St George's church on your right, you will find St Oswald's Cottages (number 3). The church, incidentally, was built in 1895; the Bluebell Inn and a thatched cottage stood here before then. Unusually, the nave of St George's runs from north to south, with the altar in the north, rather than east to west with the altar in the east. An early photograph of Wall, taken by the well known Hexham photographer and polymath JP

Detail from Gibson photograph of Wall Village (dated c. 1865) taken above the village from the east.

Gibson in 1865, clearly shows that at the time the east gable end of St Oswald's Cottages retained an external stone staircase to the upper floor (see far right of image p.141).

As mentioned above, this cottage also has an inscribed stone over its doorway, similar to that of Greenhead House although with the slightly later date of 1642: FEARE GOD 16BKTK42 IN HART, and again this date must relate to the reconstruction work that went on in the mid 17th Century. The gable ends of both cottages have original slit vents (see above left).

Although it is thought that these terraced bastles would all have had doors facing inwards, there are traces of an old door at the end of the west end of the terrace (see below left) as well as a glimpse of the original plinth.

Returning to the village, the next obvious bastle in just around the corner from the church. Stable Cottage (number 4) has a blocked up door to the first floor (see right) and has a steeper roof pitch than other houses around it. The huge and rough masonry can be seen below.

Across the green with your back to Stable Cottage you will see the back view of Town Farm house (number 5), which now faces away from the rest of the village but which presumably in its earliest form would have faced inwards as part of the defensive circuit. There is little to see, but the walls of the original house, which has been much altered, are immensely thick, and are undoubtedly very old.

Just across the green, further west and in between Stable Cottage and the back of Town Farm is the 'pant' or village water pump and trough, built in 1858.

Our next bastle (number 6) is on the opposite side of the 'main road' through Wall, immediately up the road from the Hadrian Hotel (a good place to have a break). It could be that at one time this entire line of buildings formed the western side of the green, before the buildings in between became the 'new' western boundary. Either way, these two cottages were once a bastle, and what was once the doorway to the upper floor is now a false window, seen above the new doors.

Further along again, at right angles to the main road is Penrhyn (number 7), the exterior of which is very much of the early 19th Century. This house shows no discernable trace of its ever having been a bastle, but the interior walls are very thick, and there is what appears to be a blocked slit vent in the kitchen wall inside the house. Even less bastle-like these days is Orchard House (number 8), on the opposite side of the road from Penrhyn, and like Town Farm facing the 'wrong way' if it were indeed once a bastle. The much changed exterior may be seen on *Keys to the Past*, which suggests that it was "probably originally a bastle", but there are no details offered to support the statement.

It seems very likely to me that other houses in Wall Village, old but not as old as bastles, were built where bastles once stood, completing more fully the defensive circuit. Fellfoot and Fellfoot Cottage (number 9) fall into this category. As one who lives in the village, looking over the green, I am heartily glad that these days neither Roman nor Reiver is likely to disturb our peace.

Wall Village pant (or pump)

How to find Wall Village: Take the A6079 off the A69 just west of Hexham, towards Acomb and Chollerford; Wall is a five minute drive up this road. Turn right off the main road into the village after the Hadrian Hotel.
Access: Easy parking in the village; the bastles are all within a few minutes of each other.
Footwear: No special footwear needed.

EVISTONES BASTLE VILLAGE
ROCHESTER
NY830969

As we have seen, Wall Village has survived and adapted over the centuries and is now a fairly comfortable mixture of ancient and modern. Evistones has not. It is a dramatic and moving ghost of what it was, with earthworks and stunted walls being all that now demonstrate that here was a village, made up of long houses and bastles. Some of the remains overlap, showing successive periods of building and occupation. It must be said that takes an imaginative leap to envisage the community from what remains, but that should not put you off making the visit; at the very least, on a fine day you will have stunning views of the Northumberland countryside.

As at Wall, the dwellings were grouped around a village green, and also (it seems likely) as at Wall in earlier times, the buildings were linked by a series of defensive walls. There were three bastles with long houses in between, and the best remains by far at Evistones belong to one of these bastles.

Above can be seen the view through what was the original doorway of the bastle; you can see that the walls were immensely thick. At some point a wall has been constructed about half way along the building with a door in to what has become shelter for livestock. The shape of the stone barrel vaulting can be seen very clearly. The interior of the intact half

of the bastle is coarsely built and the walls do not appear to have any vents. At the original entrance you can just make out the checks for two doors (see image above). With so little remaining at this end of the bastle, there is no evidence remaining of drawbar tunnels, although if the jambs were still in place there certainly would be.

All of the bastles once had modest enclosures (gardens or fields) attached to them. An aerial view of Evistones shows these remains very clearly, as it does the distinctive medieval ridges and furrows formed by generations of cultivation which completely surround the village (see Frodsham et al p. 105). According to Dodds, Evistones was home to two graynes, the Hedleys and the Fletchers, but by the seventeenth century only the Fletchers remained:

> The community had a bad reputation for thieving, and the expectation of just vengeance probably accounted for the unusually strong defences. Three Fletchers were tenants in 1604; they were probably executed or deported during the Border clean-up as records end then. *(Dodds, p. 337)*

How to find Evistones: Take the A696 north from Otterburn. Having passed the Redesdale Arms at Horsley you will come to Horsley Cottage and church on your right, after which there is a space to pull in. From here you can see Evistones across the valley on the hillside. The footpath begins a hundred yards further up the main road.

Access: Take the footpath down the lane to Stobbs Farm (another ancient settlement) and then follow the track round and over the bridge. The footbridge marked on the OS map is no longer there. Keep walking, past the farm buildings, and then follow the track up to the ruins, which are clearly in view.

Footwear: Stout boots or wellies

View north east from Shittleheugh

Bibliography

Titles in bold were still in print in 2008, although not necessarily in th
edition used by the author of this book, and should be available from
any good book shop.

Dodds, John F. *Bastions and Belligerents*, Keepdate Publishing, undated
but c.1999

Durham, K. *The Border Reivers*, Osprey, 1995

**Fraser, G.M. *The Steel Bonnets*, Harper Collins Trade Paperback edit.,
1995**

**Frodsham, P. et al *Archaeology in Northumberland National Park*,
Council for British Archaeology, 2004.**

Graham, A. *Notes on Some Northumbrian "Peles"*, Proceedings of the
Society of Antiquaries of Scotland Vol. LXXX pp 37-43.
This can be found by visiting the following website: **http://ads.ahds.
ac.uk/catalogue** and following the links through the **library** to the
Proceedings of the Society of Antiquaries of Scotland.

**Hugill, R. *Borderland Castles and Peles*, reprinted by Sandhill Press,
1996**

Jones, T. et al *The Melkridge Bastle, Northumberland*, in Archaeologia
Aeliana Vol. 34, 1956

Long, B. *Castles of Northumberland*, Harold Hill, 1967

Rowland, T.H. *Medieval Castles, Towers, Peles and Bastles of Northumberland,* Sandhill Press, 1994 edition

Ramm, H.G. et al Royal Commission On Historical Monuments *Shielings and Bastles,* HMSO, 1970

Ryder, P. *Bastles and Bastle-Like Buildings in Allendale, Northumberland* in the Journal of the Royal Archeological Institute 149, 1992, pp 351-379

Ryder, P. **Bastle Houses in the Northern Pennines,** North Pennines Heritage Trust, 1996

Sadler, J. **Border Fury,** Pearson Education pb edit, 2006

Tomlinson, W.W. *Comprehensive Guide to Northumberland,* Walter Scott, 1888

Trevelyan, G.M. *English Social History,* Longmans, 1946

ONLINE SOURCES

Durham and Northumberland Local Government Information: www.keystothepast.info/

Calendar of Border Papers: www.british-history.ac.uk

BASTLES